**Graphic Design:** Daniel Gelon

**Layout:** Daniel Gelon, Dave Howell, Anson Maddocks, Jesper Myrfors, Tom Wänerstrand

**Cover:** Jesper Myrfors, Daniel Gelon

**Illustrations:** Christopher Rush

**Editing:** Kathryn Haines, Dave Howell, Beverly Marshall Saling, Ken McGlothlen

**Additional Editing by:** Skaff Elias, Kathy Ice, Beth Moursund, Bronwyn Rice, Victor K. Wertz, Paul Hughes

This book would never have been possible without the assistance of countless people. Our thanks to Richard Garfield, John Jordan, Carol Monahan, Lisa Stevens, Peter Adkison, Tom Des Brisay, Dave Haas, Tom Wylie, Glenn Elliott, T. Brian Wagner, and Darlene Miller. Special thanks to people who helped critique the new rules in a very short time: Kevin Maroney, Geoffrey Speare, Peter Sarrett, Preston Kent, Ken Martin, D. K. Fenger, Mark Biggar, Anton Dovydaitis, and Nicholas J. Sauer, plus the always-remarkable efforts of the East Coast Playtesting Team—Jim Lin, Chris Page, Skaff Elias, Joel Mick, and Dave Pettey. We are also grateful to the people on electronic bulletin boards who asked the questions that showed what needed to change. Finally, we'd like to thank our distributors, customers, and the players of **Magic,** who continue to amaze us with their enthusiasm and support. Thank you all for sharing this adventure with us.

THE

# MAGIC

The Gathering™

## Pocket
## Players' Guide

with illustrations by Christopher Rush

© 1994 Wizards of the Coast, Inc. All Rights Reserved.

Printed in the United States of America. [cue Sousa]

94  95  96  97     9  8  7  6  5  4  3

ISBN 1-880992-29-9

# I

# *The Creation of Magic: The Gathering*

## •Notes from the Designer

In its ten years of development, **Magic** has undergone a remarkable evolution. Here the game's creator, Richard Garfield, muses on the design challenges of the collectable trading card game and recounts the game's eventful playtest history.

# Notes From The Designer

*Richard Garfield*

## The Ancestry of Magic

Games evolve. New ones take the most loved features of earlier games and add original characteristics. The creation of *Magic: The Gathering* is a case in point.

Though there are about a dozen games that have directly influenced **Magic** in one way or another, the game's most influential ancestor is a game for which I have no end of respect: *Cosmic Encounter*, originally published by Eon Products and re-released by Mayfair Games. In this game, participants play alien races striving to conquer a piece of the universe. Players can attempt their conquest alone, or forge alliances with other aliens. There are nearly fifty alien races which can be played, each of which has a unique ability: the Amoeba, for example, has the power to Ooze, giving it unlimited token movement; the Sniveler has the power to Whine, allowing it to automatically catch up when behind. The best thing about *Cosmic Encounter* is precisely this limitless variety. I have played hundreds of times and still can be surprised at the interactions different combinations of aliens produce. *Cosmic Encounter* remains enjoyable because it is constantly new.

*Cosmic Encounter* proved to be an interesting complement to my own design ideas. I had been mulling over a longtime idea of mine: a game which used a deck of cards whose composition changed between rounds. During the course of the game, the players would add cards to and remove cards from the deck, so that when you played a new game

# Introduction

Welcome to the world of **Magic.**

This imaginary multiverse even has a name: Dominia. It's a world of many planets, places, and planes, and we want to share it with you through the deceptively simple mechanism of a deck of cards.

When we first released *Magic: The Gathering* in August 1993, we were unprepared for the reception it received. We hoped that the game our artists, designers, writers, and playtesters were creating would appeal to our customers, and help cultivate interest in the new genre of collectable trading card games that we found so interesting. As our customers have shown, we were, if anything, *too* successful. Players are exploring the game with an enthusiasm and a depth that we never expected. They have gone to lengths we never imagined to complete their card collections, build their decks, and introduce new players to the game. **Magic** has truly taken on a life of its own.

As the players' knowledge of the game and its potential has developed, so has ours. Every day we learn things about **Magic** that we couldn't have imagined when we were playtesting it. This book is both a result of this exploration and a prompt to further efforts. A collaboration between the designers and the players, *The Pocket Players' Guide* is intended to clarify the game as it is presently understood, so that we all share common ground as we continue to explore the phenomenon that is **Magic.**

# Contents

it would have an entirely different card mix. I remembered playing marbles in elementary school, where each player had his own collection from which he would trade and compete. I was also curious about *Strat-o-matic™ Baseball*, in which participants draft, field, and compete their own teams of baseball players, whose abilities are based on real players' previous year statistics. Intrigued by the structure of the game, I was irritated that the subject was one for which I had no patience.

These thoughts were the essence of what eventually became **Magic**. My experiences with *Cosmic Encounter* and other games inspired me to create a card game in 1982 called *Five Magics*. *Five Magics* was an attempt to distill the modularity of *Cosmic Encounter* down to just a card game. The nature of *Cosmic Encounter* seemed entirely appropriate for a magical card game—wild and not entirely predictable, but not completely unknown, like a set of forces you almost, but don't quite, understand. Over the next few years, *Five Magics* went on to inspire entirely new magical card games among my friends.

Ten years later, I was still designing games, and Mike Davis and I had come up with a board game called *RoboRally*. Mike was acting as our agent, and among the companies he approached was a brand-new gaming company called Wizards of the Coast. Things seemed to be going well, so that August, Mike and I made our way to Portland, Oregon to meet over a pizza with Peter Adkison and James Hays of Wizards of the Coast.

Both Peter and James were very receptive to *RoboRally*, but informed me that they weren't really in a position to come out with a board game right away. This wasn't what I had come out to hear, of course, but I didn't want the trip to be a total waste. I asked Peter what he would be interested in. Peter replied that he really saw a need for a game that could be played quickly with minimal equipment, a game that would go over well at conventions. Could I do it?

Within a few days, the initial concept for a trading card game was born, based on another card game I had developed in 1985 called *Safecracker*. It hadn't been one of my best games. But then I remembered *Five Magics*.

## The First Designs

I went back to graduate school at the University of Pennsylvania, and worked on the card game in whatever spare time I had. It wasn't easy; there were three months of false starts on the project, there are so many aspects of card game design that have to be reconsidered when designing trading card games. First of all, you can't have any bad cards—people wouldn't play with them. In fact, you want to prevent too much range in the utility of cards because players will only play with the best—why make cards people won't play with? Besides, homogeneity of card power is the only way to combat the "rich kid syndrome" that threatened the game concept from the start. What was to keep someone from going out and getting ten decks and becoming unbeatable?

It was a major design concern. I had numerous theories on how to prevent purchasing power from unbalancing the game, none of which were entirely valid but all of which had a grain of truth. The most compelling counter to this "buy-out-the-store" strategy was the ante. If we were playing for ante, the argument ran, and your deck was the distilled fruit of ten decks, when I did win, I would win a more valuable card. Also, if the game had enough skill, then the player purchasing their power would surely be easy prey for the players dueling and trading their way to a good deck. And of course there was the sentiment that buying a lot of poker chips doesn't make you a winner. In the end, however, the "rich kid syndrome" became less of a concern. **Magic** is a fun game, and it doesn't really matter how you get your deck. Playtesting showed that a deck that is too powerful defeats itself. On the one hand, people stopped playing against it for ante unless a handicap was invoked; on the other, it inspired them to assemble more effective decks in response.

The first **Magic** release was affectionately named Alpha. It consisted of 120 cards split randomly between two players. The two players would ante a card, fight a duel over the ante, and repeat until they got bored. They often took a long time to get bored; even then, **Magic** was a surprisingly addictive game. About ten o'clock one evening, Barry "Bit" Reich and I started a game in the University of Pennsylvania Astronomy lounge, a windowless, air-conditioned room. We played continuously until about 3:00am— at least that's what we thought, until we left the building and found that the sun had risen.

I knew then that I had a game structure that could support the concept of individually owned and tailored decks. The game was quick, and while it had bluffing and strategy, it didn't seem to get bogged down with too much calculation. The various combinations that came up were enjoyable and often surprising. At the same time, the variety of card combinations didn't unbalance the game: when a person started to win, it didn't turn into a landslide.

# From Alpha to Gamma

Except for the card mix, little has changed about **Magic** since Alpha. In Alpha, walls could attack, and losing all your lands of a particular color destroyed the associated spells in play, but otherwise, the rules are much the same now as they were in the early stages of playtesting.

Moving from Alpha to the Beta version was like releasing a wild animal. The enjoyable game that was Alpha now burst the confines of the duel to invade the lives of the participants. Players were free to trade cards between games and hunt down weaker players to challenge them to duels, while gamely facing or cravenly avoiding those who were more powerful. Reputations were forged—reputations built on anything from consistently strong play to a few lucky wins to good bluffing. The players didn't know the card mix, so they learned to stay on their toes during duels. Even the most alert players would occasionally meet with nasty surprises. This constant discovery of unknown realms in an uncharted world gave the game a feeling of infinite size and possibility.

For the Gamma version, new cards were added and many of the creature costs were increased. We also doubled the pool of playtesters, adding in a group with *Strat-o-matic Baseball* experience. We were particularly anxious to find out if **Magic** could be adapted for league play. Gamma was also the first version which was fully illustrated. Skaff Elias was my art director: he and others spent days poring over old graphic magazines, comic books, and game books searching for art for the cards. These playtest decks were pretty attractive for crummy black-and-white cardstock photocopies. For the most part, the cards were illustrated with serious pictures, but there were a lot of humorous ones as well. Heal was illustrated by Skaff's foot. Power Sink showed Calvin (of "Calvin and Hobbes") in a toilet; after all, what is a toilet but a power sink? Berserk was John Travolta dancing in *Saturday Night Fever*. Righteousness pictured Captain Kirk, and Blessing showed Spock doing his "live long and prosper" gesture. An old comic book provided a Charles Atlas picture for Holy Strength, and a 98-pound weakling getting sand kicked in his face for Weakness. Instill Energy was Richard Simmons. The infamous Glasses of Urza were some X-ray glasses we found in a catalog. Ruthy Kantorovitz constructed a darling flame-belching baby for Firebreathing. I myself had the honor of being the Goblins. The pictures and additional players greatly added to the game atmosphere. It became clear that while the duels were for two players, the more players playing, the better the game was. In some sense, the individual duels were a part of a single, larger game.

## Striking the Balance

Each playtest set saw the expulsion of certain cards. One type of card that was common in Alpha and Beta was rare in Gamma, and is now nonexistent: the type that made one of your rival's cards yours. Yes, Control Magic used to permanently steal a creature from your opponent. Similarly, Steal Artifact really took an artifact. Copper Tablet no longer even remotely resembles its original purpose, which was to swap two creatures in play. ("Yes, I'll swap my Merfolk for your Dragon. On second thought, make that my Goblins—they're uglier.") There was a spell, Planeshift, which stole a land, and Ecoshift, which collected all the lands, shuffled them and redealt them—really nice for the user of four or five colors of magic. Pixies used to be a real pain—if they hit you, you swapped a random card from your hand with your opponent. These cards added something to the game, often in the form of players trying to destroy their own creatures before their opponents took them for good, or even trying to take their own lives to preserve the last shreds of their decks. However, in the end it was pretty clear that the nastiness this added to the game environment wasn't worth the trouble, and no card should ever be at risk unless players choose to play for ante.

It was around this time that I began to realize that almost any decision made about the game would be opposed, often vehemently, by some players. The huge amount of dissent about what should and should not be part of the card mix has led players to make their own versions for playtesting— a significant task that involves designing, constructing, shuffling, and distributing about 4000 cards. Each of these games had its merits, and the playtesters enjoyed discovering the quirks and secrets of each new environment. The results of these efforts will form the basis of future **Deckmaster** games that use the structure of *The Gathering*, while containing mostly new cards.

## To Build a Better Deck

Playtesting a **Deckmaster** game is difficult. Probably the only games harder to playtest are elaborate, multi-player computer games. After developing a basic framework for **Magic** that seemed fairly robust, we had to decide which of the huge selection of cards to include, and with what relative frequencies. Common cards had to be simple, but not necessarily less powerful, than rare cards—if only rare cards were powerful, players would either have to be rich or lucky to get a decent deck. Sometimes a card was made rare because it was too powerful or imbalancing in large quantities, but more often, rare cards were cards that were intricate or specialized—spells you wouldn't want many of anyway. But these design guidelines only got us so far. The whole game's flavor could change if a handful of seemingly innocent cards were eliminated, or even made less or more common. When it came down to actually deciding what to include and what to do without, I began to feel like a chef obliged to cook a dish for 10,000 people using 300 ingredients.

One thing I knew I wanted to see in the game was players using multicolor decks. It was clear that a player could avoid a lot of problems by stripping down to a single color. For this reason, many spells were included that paralyzed entire colors, like Karma, Elemental Blast, and the Circles of Protection. The original plan was to include cards that thwarted every obvious simple strategy, and, in time, to add new cards which would defeat the most current ploys and keep the strategic environment dynamic. For example, it was obvious that relying on too many big creatures made a player particularly vulnerable to the Meekstone, and a deck laden with Fireballs and requiring lots of mana could be brought down with Manabarbs. Unfortunately, this strategy and counter-strategy design led to players developing narrow decks and refusing to play people who used cards that could defeat them flat out. If players weren't compelled to play a variety of players and could choose their opponent every time, a narrow deck was pretty powerful.

Therefore, another, less heavy-handed way to encourage variety was developed. We made it more difficult to get all the features a player needs in a deck by playing a single color. Gamma, for example, suffered from the fact that blue magic could stand alone. It was easily the most powerful magic, having two extremely insidious common spells (Ancestral Memory and Time Walk), both of which have been made rare. It had awesome counterspell capabilities. It had amazing creatures, two of the best of which are now uncommon.

Blue magic now retains its counterspell capability, but is very creature poor, and lacks a good way to do direct damage. Red magic has little defense, particularly in the air, but has amazing direct damage and destruction capability. Green magic has an abundance of creatures and mana, but not much more. Black is the master of anticreature magic and has some flexibility, but is poorly suited to stopping noncreature threats. White magic is the magic of protection, and the only magic with common banding, but has little damage-dealing capability.

Sometimes seemingly innocuous cards would combine into something truly frightening. A good part of playtest effort was devoted to routing out the cards that contributed to so-called "degenerate" decks—the narrow, powerful decks that are difficult to beat and often boring to play with or against. Without a doubt, the most striking was Tom Fontaine's "Deck of Sooner-Than-Instant Death," which was renowned for being able to field upwards of eight large creatures on the second or third turn. In the first **Magic** tournament, Dave "Hurricane" Pettey walked to victory with his "Land Destruction Deck." (Dave also designed a deck of Spectres, Mindtwists, and Disrupting Sceptres that was so gruesome I don't think anyone was ever really willing to play it.) Skaff's deck, "The Great White Death," could out-live just about anything put up against it. Charlie Catin's "Weenie Madness" was fairly effective at swamping the opponent with little creatures. Though this deck was probably not in the high-win bracket of the previous decks, it was recognized that, playing for ante, Charlie could hardly lose. Even winning only one in four of his games—and he could usually do better than that—the card he won could be traded back for the island and the two Merfolk he lost, with something extra thrown in.

In the end I decided that the degenerate decks were actually part of the fun. People would assemble them, play with them until they got bored or their regular opponents refused to play against them, and then retire the deck or trade off its components for something new—a **Magic** version of putting the champion out to stud. Most players ended up treating their degenerate decks much like roleplayers treat their most successful characters: they were relegated to the background, to be occasionally dusted off for a new encounter.

After the pursuit of sheer power died down, another type of deck developed: the Weird Theme deck. These decks were usually made to be as formidable as possible within the constraints of their theme. When Bit grew bored of his "Serpent Deck" (he had a predilection for flopping a rubber snake on the playing surface and going "SsssSssSs" whenever he summoned a Serpent), he developed his "Artifact Deck," which consisted of artifacts only—no land. It was fun to see the "Artifact Deck" go up against someone who used Nevinyrral's Disk. But the king of weird decks was, without a doubt, Charlie Catin. In one league, he put together a deck that I call "The Infinite Recursion Deck." The idea was to set up a situation where his opponent couldn't attack him until Charlie could play Swords to Plowshares on a creature. Then he would play Timetwister, causing the cards in play to be shuffled with the graveyard, hand, and library to form a fresh library. Swords to Plowshares actually removes a creature from the game, so his rival has one less creature. Repeat. After enough iterations, his rival was bloated with life given by the Swords to Plowshares, having maybe 60 life points, but there were no creatures left in his deck. So Charlie's Elves started in—59 life, 58 life, 57 life—and the curtain closes on this sad game. I still can't think about this deck without moist emotional snorts. The *coup de grace* is that this league required players to compete their decks ten times. And, since his games often lasted over an hour and a half, he received at least one concession.

## Words, Words, Words

It was not just determining the right card mix that players and designers found challenging. This becomes increasingly clear to me as I participate in the never-ending process of editing the rules and the cards. As my earliest playtesters have pointed out (in their more malicious moods,) the original concept for **Magic** was the simplest game in the world because you had all the rules on the cards. That notion is long gone.

To those who didn't have to endure it, our struggle for precision was actually rather amusing. My own rules discussions about card wordings were mostly with Jim Lin, who is the closest thing you will ever encounter to a combination rules lawyer and firehose. A typical rule-problem session would go:

Jim:        Hmm—there seems to be a problem with this card. Here is my seven-page rules addition to solve the problem.

Richard:    I would sooner recall all the cards than use that. Let's try this solution instead.

Jim:    Hmm—we have another problem.

[*Repeat until . . .* ]

Richard:  This is silly—only incredibly stupid and terminally anal people could *possibly* misinterpret this card.

Jim:    Yes, maybe we *have* been thinking about this too long. If you're playing with that kind of person, you should find some new friends.

A specific example of something we actually worried about is whether Consecrate Land would really protect your land from Stone Rain. After all, the first says it prevents land from being destroyed and the second says it destroys the land. Isn't that a contradiction? It still hurts my head getting into a frame of mind where that is confusing. It is perhaps a little like wondering why anyone would give you anything for money, which is, after all, just paper.

But, then again, I could never tell what was going to confuse people. One of the playtesters, Mikhail Chkhenkeli, approached me and said, "I like my deck. I have the most powerful card in the game. When I play it, I win on the next turn." I tried to figure out what this could be; I couldn't think of anything that would win the game with any assurance the turn after casting. I asked him about it and he showed me a card that would make his opponent skip a turn. I was confused until I read exactly what was written: "Opponent loses next turn." It was my first real lesson in how difficult it was going to be to word the cards so that no two people would interpret the same card in a different way.

# The Magic Marketplace

Another thing I realized in the second year of playtesting really surprised me. **Magic** turned out to be one of the best economic simulations I had ever seen. We had a free-market economy and all of the ingredients for interesting dynamics. People valued different cards in different ways—sometimes because they simply weren't evaluating accurately, but much more often because the cards really have different value to different players. For example, the value of a powerful green spell was lower for a person who specializes in black and red magic than for one who was building a deck that was primarily green. This gives a lot of opportunity for arbitrage. I would frequently find cards that one group of players weren't using but another group were treating like chunks of gold. If I was fast enough, I could altruistically benefit both parties and only have to suffer a little profit in the process.

Sometimes the value of a card would fluctuate based on a new use (or even a suspected new use). For example, when Charlie was collecting all the available spells that produced black mana, we began to get concerned—those cards were demanding higher and higher prices, and people began to fear what he could need all that black mana for. And, prior to Dave's "Land Destruction Deck," land destruction spells like Stone Rain and Ice Storm were not high-demand spells. This of course allowed him to assemble the deck cheaply, and after winning the first **Magic** tournament, sell off the pieces for a mint.

Trade embargoes appeared. At one point a powerful faction of players would not trade with Skaff, or anyone who traded with Skaff. I actually heard conversations such as:

Player 1 to Player 2: I'll trade you card A for card B.

> Skaff, watching: That's a moronic trade. I'll give you card B and cards C, D, E and F for card A.

> Players 1 and 2 together: We are *not* trading with *you*, Skaff.

Needless to say, Skaff was perhaps a bit *too* successful in his early duels and trades.

Another interesting economic event would occur when people would snatch up cards they had no intention of using. They would take them to remove them from the card pool, either because the card annoyed them ( Chaos Orb, for example) or because it was too deadly against their particular decks.

I think my favorite profit was turned during an encounter with Ethan Lewis and Bit. Ethan had just received a pack of cards and Bit was interested in trading with Ethan. Bit noticed that Ethan had the Jayemdae Tome, began to drool, and made an offer for it. I looked at the offer and thought it was far too low, so I put the same thing on the table.

Bit looked at me and said, "You can't offer that! If you want the Tome you have to bid higher than my bid."

I said, "This isn't an offer for the Tome. This is a gift for Ethan deigning to even discuss trading the Tome with me."

Bit looked at me in disbelief, and then took me aside. He whispered, "Look, I'll give you this wad of cards if you just leave the room for ten minutes." I took his bribe, and he bought the Tome. It was just as well—

he had a lot more buying power than I did. In retrospect, it was probably a dangerous ploy to use against Bit—after all, he was the person who was responsible for gluing poor Charlie's deck together once, washing a different deck of Charlie's in soap and water, and putting more cards of Charlie's in the blender and hitting frappé.

Probably the most constant card-evaluation difference I had with anyone was over Lord of the Pit. I received it in just about every playtest release we had, and it was certainly hard to use. I didn't agree with Skaff, though, that the only value of the card was that you might get your opponent to play with it. He maintained that blank cards would be better to play with because blank cards probably wouldn't hurt you. I argued that if you knew what you were doing, you could profit from it.

Skaff asked me to cite a single case where it had saved me. I thought a bit and recalled the most flamboyant victory I had with it. My opponent knew he had me where he wanted me—he had something doing damage to me, and a Clone in hand, so even if I cast something to turn the tide, he would be able to match me. Well, of course, the next cast spell was a Lord of the Pit; he could Clone it or die from it, so he Cloned it. Then each time he attacked, I would heal both of the Lords, or cast Fog and nullify the assault, and refuse to attack. Eventually, he ran out of creatures to keep his Lord of the Pit sated and died a horrible death.

Skaff was highly amused by this story. He said, "So, when asked about a time the Lord of the Pit saved you, you can only think of a case where you were playing somebody stupid enough to clone it!"

# Dominia and the Role of Roleplaying

Selecting a card mix that accommodated different evaluations of the cards wasn't enough; we also had to develop an environment in which the cards could reasonably interact. Establishing the right setting for **Magic** proved to be a central design challenge. In fact, many of our design problems stemmed from an attempt to define the physics of a magical world in which duels take place and from building the cards around that, rather than letting the game define the physics. I was worried about the cards' relationship to each other—I wanted them to seem part of a unified setting, but I didn't want to restrict the creativity of the designers or to create all the cards myself. Everyone trying to jointly build a single fantasy world seemed difficult, because it would inevitably lack cohesion. I preferred the idea of a *multiverse*, a system of worlds that was incredibly large and permitted strange interactions between the universes in it. In this way, we could capture the other-worldly aspects of fantasy that add such flavor to the game while preserving a coherent, playable game structure. Almost any card or concept would fit into a multiverse. Also, it would not be difficult to accommodate an ever-growing and diverse card pool—expansion sets with very different flavors could be used in the same game, for they could be seen as a creative mingling of elements from different universes. So I developed the idea of Dominia, an infinite system of planes through which wizards travel in search of resources to fuel their magic.

In its structured flexibility, this game environment is much like a roleplaying world. I don't mean to suggest that this setting makes **Magic** a roleplaying game—far from it—but **Magic** is closer to roleplaying than any other card or board game I know of. I have always been singularly unimpressed by games that presumed to call themselves a cross between the two because roleplaying has too many characteristics that can't be captured in a different format. In fact, in its restricted forms—as a tournament game or league game, for example—**Magic** has little in common with roleplaying. In those cases, it is a game in the traditional sense, with each player striving to achieve victory according to some finite set of rules. However, the more free-form game—dueling with friends using decks constructed at whim—embodies some interesting elements of roleplaying.

Each player's deck is like a character. It has its own personality and quirks. These decks often even get their own names: "The Bruise," "The Reanimator," "Weenie Madness," "Sooner-Than-Instant Death," "Walk Into This Deck," "The Great White Leftovers," "Backyard Barbeque," and "Gilligan's Island," to name a few. In one deck I maintained, each of the creatures had a name—one small advantage to crummy photocopied cardstock is the ease of writing on cards. The deck was called "Snow White and the Seven Dwarves," containing a Wurm named Snow White and seven Mammoths: Doc, Grumpy, Sneezy, Dopey, Happy, Bashful, and Sleepy. After a while I got a few additional Mammoths, which I named Cheesy and Hungry. There was even a Prince Charming: my Veteran Bodyguard.

As in roleplaying, the object of the game in the unstructured mode of play is determined largely by the players. The object of the duel is usually to win, but the means to that end can vary tremendously. Most players find that the duel itself quickly becomes a fairly minor part of the game compared to trading and assembling decks.

Another characteristic of **Magic** which is reminiscent of roleplaying is the way players are exploring a world rather than knowing all the details to start. I view **Magic** as a vast game played among all the people who buy decks, rather than just a series of little duels. It is a game for tens of thousands in which the designer acts as a gamemaster. The gamemaster decides what the environment will be, and the players explore that environment. This is why there are no marketed lists of cards when the cards are first sold: discovering the cards and what they do is an integral part of the game.

And like a roleplaying game, the players contribute as much to an exciting adventure as the gamemaster. To all the supporters of **Magic,** and especially to my playtesters, I am extraordinarily grateful. Without them, if this product existed at all, it would certainly be inferior. Every one of them left a mark, if not on the game itself, then in the game's lore. Any players today that have even a tenth of the fun I had playing the test versions with them will be amply pleased with **Magic**.

# II

# *The World of Dominia*

## •Dominia and Its Walkers

Richard Garfield speculates on the nature of the multiverse in which **Magic** is set, and the remarkable abilities of its inhabitants.

## •Roreca's Tale

The wizard Worzel and her furry companion face an old nemesis.

# Dominia and Its Walkers

*Richard Garfield*

Imagine a vast beach. The sand shifts constantly, moved mostly by the tide and the wind, but also by the creatures that scurry across it or burrow beneath. Subtler effects, like compression or changes in temperature, also make their mark. Sometimes the grains cling together, weathering as a single stone until they are broken apart by some other force.

Now imagine that each of these grains of sand is its own world, and you begin to get a picture of how Dominia works. Dominia is a multiverse, a collection of universes. Usually, the inhabitants of a particular world have no inter-action with the other universes; they live out their lives believing that their home is the "One World." Even when some cataclysm on a nearby plane affects the surrounding worlds, the occupants of those worlds can blame the gods, or perhaps invent nonexistent natural laws to explain the changes in their plane.

A small number of the multiverse's inhabitants, however, are fully aware of the existence of worlds outside their home plane. These planewalkers, often called wizards, have learned to travel between planes. Most have also developed secret methods of tapping the resources of one plane for use in another. Wizards covet the special resources of the vari-ous worlds, and rich worlds are guarded jealously.

The simplest form of planewalking is travel between touching planes. If two planes in Dominia touch, a wizard familiar with both planes can usually travel from anywhere on one of the planes to some location on the other. Of course, experienced wizards can control where they arrive better than less experienced ones can. A planewalker can also travel between planes that don't touch each other by walking through a potentially long series of intermediate planes that span the gap. Distance between two planes can be approximated by the number of intermediate worlds travelled through. Since travel between planes is rapid, even trips to extremely distant planes can be quick. However, if the region is unfamiliar or the paths between planes even slightly unstable, the wizard may accidentally travel far astray or become lost. For this reason, planewalkers traversing unfamiliar or shifting paths will take their time to make sure they are going to the correct plane each step of the way.

Even experienced planewalkers cannot easily predict how the paths between planes will form and change. Some areas of Dominia remain in the same configuration for ages, and the paths that bind them shift only slightly. Others are in constant turmoil, making walking between worlds perilous. Sometimes a set of planes will crystallize, like sandstone on the beach; in these cases, travel between the united planes stabilizes, but the entire region may shift in relation to the rest of Dominia. Planewalkers have been known to disappear entirely if the universe they currently inhabit relocates radically, or shifts free of Dominia itself.

Each plane has its own laws, though these can change as the plane shifts into new regions. Some planes have no domestic magic at all: wizards travelling in these regions must draw entirely on extraplanar resources. Others are so replete with magic that the occupants can be dangerous even to wizards with the forces of many planes at their call. Planewalkers who spend a great deal of time on a particular plane can often master the laws that govern it, allowing them to control the plane or at least tap its resources more effectively.

The resources of a plane can be called upon by lines which connect to that plane. These are invisible except to one who knows how to perceive them. The lines carried by a typical wizard will connect to many worlds of Dominia. The lines which provide wizards with raw energy for their spells, the mana lines, usually connect to the lands of the various planes. Lands in most parts of Dominia can be divided into five basic types, each of which provides energy for a different kind of magic. There is white mana, stemming from the more serene lands of the planes, which enables the magic of order, protection, and construction. There is black mana, bubbling forth from the more corrupt lands of the planes, and powers the magic of ruin, death, and decay. Green mana emanates from the wild lands and generates the magic of life and nature. From the oceans and islands of Dominia's planes comes blue mana, fueling the magic of artifice, water, and air. Finally there is red mana, drawn from the mountainous regions, which drives the magic of destruction and chaos. Other lines will link to the wizards' minions, spells, or to artifacts from other worlds whose powers the wizards can drawn on. A wizard uses the energy provided by the mana lines to call upon these other resources.

Lines will fade and become unreliable at great distances from the source; at extreme distances, they can vanish altogether. Extreme care is practiced by wizards that deal with these lines for any length of time. The others die out. The lines carry the power of worlds.

Planewalkers answer to no higher authority, for no code of law is enforceable. You can't restrain a wizard because wizards can leave the plane they are on at any time. You can't banish a wizard because you can't effectively keep a wizard from entering a plane. Killing a wizard is possible but difficult, since at a moments notice the intended victim could be a dozen planes away. Once they flee you have no hope of tracking them through all the shifting worlds of Dominia. Even if you do manage to kill one there is no guarantee that a wizard will stay dead. Wizards have been known to plan for even that contingency, creating completely new bodies when their old ones are destroyed.

Planewalkers tend to be individualistic and territorial. While there is some collusion between wizards, and even a political structure of sorts in certain areas of Dominia, these are as unstable as the paths between planes. Occasionally lesser wizards will form alliances to prevent more experienced hands from seizing anything of value. Just as often, though, these inexperienced wizards will search on their own for lines in out-of-the-way planes. Occasionally the more enterprising or foolhardy among them will attempt to jump another wizard's claim, but the results are unpredictable. They may have the stealth and speed to avoid a confrontation, but they often sacrifice control of the claim, and lose their own lines in the process. Yet no matter how inexperienced they are, no wizard can be taken lightly. They are travellers of the multiverse; only they can fully explore its infinite planes and harness its vast, unpredictable power.

Anything you can conceive of can be found in Dominia— but it is as hard to find as a specific grain of sand on an ever-shifting beach. And in your search you will have to contend with the planewalkers, who, while not numerous, have a very wide influence.

# Roreca's Tale

*Richard Garfield*

The Ergamon plane did not impress her with its colossal peaks and exotic fauna. Of course, "colossal" and "exotic" are nearly meaningless words to Worzel, because they presume everything else in Dominia is "average" or "normal," which is not an assumption Worzel makes by now. So I suppose it is no surprise that she wasn't impressed. I was, though.

Ergamon is a small, hidden plane. At least that is what Worzel told me, though it looked as vast as any other world I had visited. I have no idea what she means by hidden. For me a hidden place is a hole-in-the-wall tavern where I can escape attention, or a woodland grotto obscured by the surrounding forest. For someone who has ways of seeing and travelling between worlds like Worzel, maybe planes can be "hidden" in the same way. But what would obscure a wizard's sight when she can see from plane to plane? Some sort of plane-forest? Thinking about what Worzel means usually makes my head ache, so I've learned to stop worrying about it.

We were standing near the bottom of a ravine between two of the Ergamon mountains. The breeze was dry and subtly scented. The base of the mountain met the ravine in a craggy black cliff slick with trickling streams. About a hundred feet away on the ravine floor we could see what appeared to be a dry river bed.

Worzel was examining the ruins of a structure built of shiny black rock. Each stone was as large as a horse. Occasionally she would mutter some incantation, or pull some weird instrument out of thin air which she would pass over the rock. When she was satisfied, the instrument would disappear. Planewalkers can travel light.

We came to Ergamon to seek lines. Wizards use lines to connect to the lands of the planes, from which they draw most of their power. Once we find a line Worzel establishes a bond to it, and then she can draw on that bond for mana. Finding the lines is my job. I am good at it; I think that's because I am built so close to the ground.

Occasionally we come across something else she is interested in, like a device or place or maybe a creature of some type. Or a pile of black stones. I can never predict what will interest her and what she will pass by. Sometimes she will spend days examining something and then leave without a comment. At other times she will give a shout and show me a kaleidescope of colors emitting from her hand, or a pool of some sparking liquid, or sometimes something I can't even see. She says that these things have lines like the land lines, and that she bonds with them too. I don't usually ask her what these lines do for her anymore. Sometimes I understand her response, but more often I nod and wag my tail as she tries to express something I can't comprehend. Sometimes she'll flush a little while explaining; I suspect that even she isn't sure what all the lines can do.

I was resting, half napping, beside the stone heap. Worzel was sitting beside me reading a parchment she had pulled from nowhere, when my fur began to stand on end. I started with surprise—her warning field had just activated. That usually meant another wizard was near by, which also meant there was going to be trouble.

I have a theory about why wizards fight so much. When whelps are together they fight. We call it play fighting, but it can get pretty serious. The thing is, they can't hurt each other too badly. Their second set of teeth haven't come in yet, the male's acid sacs still contain water and the females haven't hit their growth spurt. I think wizards fight a lot because they can't really hurt each other too badly either. With an infinite number of places to flee to and their personal magic to protect them, wizards can't suffer much direct harm.

Worzel, though, would probably say she fights to protect her domain. Her precious lines are threatened with other planewalkers around. She would also say she has to fight because they attack her. That's true, and she attacks them in anticipation of this. Planewalkers do make friends with each other, but the paths to friendship are like the paths between planes: unstable and often violent. Worzel's best friends are old duel opponents.

I had only been through a few duels by then, and Worzel had told me that if I didn't stay close by she might not be able to keep me shielded or bring me with her if she was forced to flee. She also told me that if I were constantly underfoot she would toss me out herself, even though I weigh about three times as much as she does. So I wasn't sure just how far away from her I should get at a time like this.

She gestured and pulled a handful of lichen-covered dirt out of nowhere. The dirt clod was dripping water, and the lichen looked like miniature trees, over which hung a tiny rainbow. I glanced up and saw a real rainbow in the distance. I swung my head to see more clearly: a hand-sized map showed rivers flowing between her fingers, and tiny mountain lakes reflecting cloudlets. She sighed. "Thomil." Her sigh made me shiver. I knew Thomil was another planewalker, and a powerful one, from what Worzel had said.

I peered closer at her clump of dirt, trying to see Thomil. Worzel glared at me and blew across the top of the map, raising a cloud of dust which made me back off, sneezing.

Letting go of the clod, she reached in front of her with both hands, as if she were preparing to play an unseen harp. I had seen this before: she was gathering her lines for battle. You could tell by the way her fingers and hands would disappear and reappear quickly, with a flicker. Soon I saw some of the land lines in her hands. She took some of the lines and began to braid them. I can see why wizards don't keep their lines braided all the time so they can always draw on their power. The energies that crackle through the lines are immense, even to those standing close by, let alone to the wizard holding the lines in hand. It would be like leaving a teapot always boiling so you could make tea anytime. Except that the wizard is the teapot.

Worzel pulled at the air with one hand as if yanking an invisible rope. There was a crack and out of the air fell half a dozen little winged people. "Scryb," I thought, and backed away. They hit the ground and dusted themselves off, buzzing angrily among themselves. The cloying odor of slightly aged marigolds hung in the air. One of the Scryb pointed at me and said "Kawa buje nor Ro-ree-ka Kamf," rolling the 'r's like Scryb do, and they all laughed. I am not sure what it means, but that's what they call me: "Roreca Kamf," which means Roreca Blanket. I don't like Scryb; once some of them stole a square foot of my back fur for a coverlet. Worzel fixed it, but it hurt like a thousand ironburs, and since her healing magic is not as good as perhaps it could be, I have a tattoo there rather than fur. Worzel snapped her fingers and a glowfly appeared. The Scryb were still laughing noisily but she looked at them sharply and they were quiet. Worzel waved her hand and the glowfly went speeding off with the Scryb following it. The glowfly would guide the Scryb to where Worzel wanted them to go. I hoped they wouldn't come back— the Scryb usually don't.

Worzel yanked again and pulled an enormous bear from nowhere, bringing with it the cool, musty smell of deep forest. It reared up  briefly on two legs and then went back down on four and flared its nostrils at us. Shortly after that another bear appeared. The bears followed their own glowflies. There aren't any bears or Scryb native to Ergamon, but since Worzel didn't have any lines to local creatures she used creatures from other planes.

I noticed that Worzel had a blue land line in her hand which she hadn't woven. I hoped she didn't braid it in. The last duel we were besieged by huge sea snakes, which Worzel says gained access to the plane we occupied through the land line itself. All I know is that she wove the line in and suddenly the world was titanic teeth and scales and a cold black eye as large across as I am. I looked at the land lines she had woven: several green lines and a red one. The green lines are where the Scryb and the bears would have come from. The red line could explain the flashes off in the distance and rolling  thunder. I watched the line fade to a dark red and slowly grow brighter to the sound of the thunder, like an artery filling with blood.

I was wondering what Thomil was doing, when Worzel inhaled sharply. "Black magic," I heard her mutter with surprise and what seemed like disappointment. Then a sound burst from far beyond the nearest crag, a wail that made me cower and shiver: the cry of a bear being terrified to death. I found myself howling before I could restrain myself. Worzel looked grim but said nothing, focusing on her lines.

I could smell it before it came into sight down the ravine, something rotten. Even Worzel seemed to choke on the stench for a moment. Creatures began to shamble up the slope toward the clearing in which we stood. I couldn't tell whether they had once gone on four legs or two, or perhaps three; I could tell only that these beasts no longer lived, they just moved. I saw their progress falter and stop. The walking dead gnashed their teeth and swiped their claws at the invisible barriers that kept them at bay. Worzel betrayed signs of pain as they struggled to close the gap; it was costly for her to repel the decaying things herself.

"Where are you, Cabralin Shire?" I heard her complain, as she did some more weaving. Cabralin was where we were shortly before Ergamon, a peaceful plane with lots of rolling hills and fields. The shire was the area where I found a white line. I noticed she had braided in the blue line, and I looked nervously around for signs of the snakes. She gestured toward the sky and dark clouds began to gather, and the wind picked up. She pointed at the dead still struggling up the hill, and they flew up into the air leaving a small hail of torn clothing and teeth. I saw them get sucked into the storm which was now raging high in the sky. "Sorry my little sprites," muttered Worzel. I guess they got sucked into the storm also.

The storm began to abate, and I relaxed a little. The wind had cleared the stench of the grave, and the sun came out again. I wondered if both bears had perished or just the one whose death cry I had heard. Worzel was still muttering about her missing white line, and about the protection she'd have if she found it, when she suddenly quieted and froze. She looked off into the distance and began to turn pale. She glanced anxiously at the floating clod, and went back to her weaving with redoubled effort. I was terrified. I looked at the map and saw a dark shadow hanging off to one side . The air began to stink again—not as strong as the walking dead, but much more corrupt. And I suspected the source of the smell was still far away.

A wild gibbering echoed from down the ravine, and up the hill came bounding a lanky, hunched man-thing. Worzel didn't look like she was even paying attention. At first I was relieved that the threat was so small. But the man-thing's scent was not the same as the corrupt smell that came from over the mountains. In fact, the stench was now so strong that I could barely make out the scent of the creature clawing its way through Worzel's barriers. Worzel snapped an invisible rope and out of nowhere fell more sprites. I concealed my disappointment. She created a glowfly for them to follow, and sent them off over the mountain, confirming my fear that the real threat hadn't yet arrived.

The sun was blotted out as a solid, spreading darkness came over the mountain. The stench was overpowering. The cries of the man-thing were drowned in the beating of enormous wings. When the darkness landed, the ground shook so hard that rocks broke from the cliff and fell about us. The creature stood in the riverbed down the hill, but its head was level with us. It was some type of demon, the skin blackened and bathed in patches of flame. From its huge fists, with nails the size of plows, fell the charred remains of the sprites.

Heat struck me as the demon strode up the hill; small trees and bushes on the hillside burst into flame as it past. The man-thing still yammered and clawed before us, cowed by this new terror. Crushing the beast in its left hand, the demon tore at the limp body with its teeth. "Well, that's one problem solved," I thought, hysterically. "Thomil, you fool, you fool!" cried Worzel. "The Pitlord! I can't believe you can be this stupid!" The demon raised both fists above its head, the remains of the man-thing dangling from its mouth. It brought them down on us with such force that

Worzel was thrown to the ground even under the protective fields. I heard her scream in pain. I howled. Gasping, she scrambled to her knees and began to gesture frantically. I shut my eyes and pressed myself flat against the ground. Perhaps the Pitlord wouldn't notice me. Not that it mattered; if Worzel died, I was as good as gone anyhow. I wondered which of us the Pitlord would eat first.

I could hear Worzel beside me, mumbling something, in a last desperate attempt to fight off the demon. The footfalls of the Pitlord made the ground tremble, and the stench was paralyzing. Worzel shouted; I wanted to run, but fear held me frozen. It took me a moment to realize that she was laughing. "Thomil, you fool, you wonderful fool!" I opened my eyes and saw her smiling at her hands. Some of her land lines were changing color, fading from pink to white. "Rubbing it in by denying me mountain forces, Thomil? I guess you don't know I have been brushing up on my white magic." She spun in a circle as the Pitlord brought its fists down again. This time they met a shield of white flame which formed over our heads. The Pitlord howled in surprise and pain. The heat stopped, the sound lessened, and even the smell faded as a glowing membrane of light surrounded us. Outside I could hear the Pitlord raging, but I couldn't feel even a tremor as it clawed at the edges of our sphere of light. Wherever it touched the sphere sparks flew and white flame sizzled.

The Pitlord bellowed, but it seemed distant. Worzel watched it intently, fingering her land lines. Frustrated by the impenetrable light which surrounded us, the Pitlord soon gave up the attack. Spreading its huge wings, the demon launched itself upward and flew off over the mountain. Worzel looked pleased with herself. She returned to the still-floating clod and watched as the patch of darkness moved from the center back to the edge. "Poor Thomil. You should be careful what you play with."

I guessed then that the duel was over and that Worzel had won. The glow faded, and Worzel scrambled out of the ravine. I followed her, reluctantly; without the sphere to protect us, I wasn't sure that the Pitlord wouldn't come back. Worzel noticed me lagging behind and smiled. "Don't worry, Roreca," she smiled. "It won't be long before Thomil is forced to abandon the plane, and I am sure he will spend ages healing. Meanwhile it's time to claim the spoils of victory." I knew what that meant. Often when a wizard is banished from a plane in the heat of battle they leave behind lines untended. We headed over the mountains to Thomil's last location. We could have gotten there much faster if Worzel had used magic, but she seemed to enjoy the climb. She was thinking about something, something that excited her.

The Pitlord raged about for a while, but eventually got bored of venting its anger on the Ergamon wildlife and scenery: when I looked at Worzel's map a few hours later, the dark spot had vanished. A thick, oily smoke hung in the air for the remainder of the day. When we arrived at the place Thomil had last stood, we saw only a steaming, hissing crater. I couldn't find any land lines. Still, more must have happened in the duel with Thomil than his defeat, because Worzel didn't even seem disappointed. "I think that it's time for another trip to Cabralin, Roreca," she said.

# III

# *Playing the Game*

## •Sequence of Play: A Quick Reference Guide

For those familiar with **Magic**, here is a short summary of the turn sequence under the Revised Edition rules.

## •*Magic: The Gathering* Revised Edition Rules

Containing a sample game and extensive examples, the revised rules clarify areas of the original rules and make a few improvements to the game.

## •Differences Between First Edition and Revised Edition Rules

For players used to First Edition cards and rules, Beth Moursund highlights the major changes between the editions.

## Sequence of Play: A Quick Reference Guide

Each player's turn consists of the following seven phases conducted in order:

**1. Untap.** You must untap all of your cards, unless you are specifically prevented from doing so by existing effects. No fast effects can be played.

**2. Upkeep.** This is an accounting phase. All effects or damage that happen "at the beginning of your turn" or "during upkeep" occur here. If any cards require action during upkeep, the player whose turn it is chooses the order in which upkeep effects occur. Fast effects are permitted.

**3. Draw.** You must draw a card. If you cannot draw a card because your library is empty, you lose. Fast effects are permitted during this phase.

**4. Main.** The main phase consists of three types of actions, taken in order: you may cast all types of spells, you may play one land card, and you may make one attack with creatures. Casting spells or playing land may occur before or after the attack; however, during the attack, only fast effects are permitted.

**5. Discard.** If you have more then seven cards, you must discard until you have only seven. If you have seven or fewer, you may not discard even if you want to. Fast effects are permitted.

**6. End.** Tell your opponent that you are finished. This is the last chance for either player to use fast effects this turn.

**7. Heal creatures.** All damage to creatures is removed automatically. All fast effects expire.

# MAGIC: THE GATHERING REVISED EDITION RULES

## Game Description

*Magic: The Gathering* is a game of battle in which you and your opponent represent powerful sorcerers attempting to drive each other from the lands of Dominia. Your deck holds your tools: creatures, land, spells, and artifacts. Careful consideration of strategy will play a significant part in the outcome. If you win, you'll gain more than mere satisfaction—the winner of a **Magic** duel also ends up with a card from the loser's deck. Over time, decks will grow and shrink, both from winning and losing cards and from trading with other **Magic** players. Such trading sessions can be very profitable, as you trade cards you don't need as much for those that strengthen your deck. Setting up a good deck configuration between games can contribute as much to winning as good tactics during a game.

Be especially careful when playing new opponents. They will probably have cards you've never seen before, and new ways of playing old ones. Even old rivals may have gained new cards and learned new tricks since the last time you met them. Dominia is a vast place, and surprises will appear long after you think you've seen it all.

## Equipment

You and your opponent will each need a deck of **Magic** cards and some way of keeping score. The most common method is pencil and paper. Some people use twenty-sided dice, turning them so that the score is face-up; others use counters or just keep score in their heads. If you're going to use counters or dice, keep in mind that many cards may end up giving you more life points than you started with. You'll also need a reasonably large, flat area on which to lay out the cards during play.

# A Sample Game

The object of the game is to drive your opponent from the land of Dominia. You each start with 20 life points, and whoever pushes the other person to zero or below first wins. You also win if your opponent cannot draw a card when required to do so.

Let's walk through a typical first game. Because we'll be doing a lot of explaining, it will seem to go somewhat slowly. Your first couple of games will probably be the same way. Once you know your deck a little better, the flow of the game should be pleasantly rapid.

You shuffle your deck while your opponent does the same. If you're playing for *ante*, you will cut her deck while she cuts yours, and you'll both turn over the top cards of each other's decks and set them aside as the ante cards. Whoever wins this game will keep both cards.

Now the two of you determine who goes first. Play scissors-paper-stone, flip a coin—whatever works. For this example, assume your adversary wins. To begin, you both draw seven cards. For her first move, your opponent draws a card, puts a *land card* down—an island—and indicates that she's done.

Your turn. You draw a card and examine your hand more closely. You'll need *mana* to cast any spells, and lands are the most common sources of mana, so you look for those first. You decide to play your forest card, a land that can generate one point of green mana. You also have a Summon Scryb Sprites spell in your hand, and it only costs one point of green mana. You know the casting cost because the Scryb Sprites card shows a single circle with a tree-like thing in it in the upper right corner; this circle matches the symbol on the forest card. One mana symbol means 1 mana point of that type. So you announce that you're drawing mana from the forest into your *mana pool*, and you turn the forest card sideways to show that you've used it this turn. Turning a card sideways is called *tapping*.

Now you've got a point of green mana loose in your mana pool. You put down the Sprites, which uses up that mana. Like all creatures, the Sprites cannot attack the turn in which they are summoned. Your turn is over, so you tell your opponent you're done.

Your opponent draws another card and puts down a second land card—a swamp. She now has a swamp and an island in play. She decides to *summon* Drudge Skeletons. The corner of this card says **1** 💀 . The skull, the symbol for black mana, matches the swamp card. The gray circle around the 1 means that one other point of mana is required, but the color of the other mana isn't important. Your adversary turns both the swamp and the island cards sideways, then uses the point of black and point of blue mana in her mana pool to cast the Skeletons summon. She indicates she's done.

At the beginning of your turn, you first untap any cards you have tapped. So you straighten out your forest card and draw a card.

You place the second land card in your hand down on the table. This time it's a plains card, which will provide white mana. You also happen to have Holy Strength in your hand. Holy Strength is an *enchant creature* card that costs 1 white mana. You tap the plains card to show you've released the mana from it, then place the Holy Strength card on your Sprites. In the lower right of the Sprites card is the notation 1/1, which indicates the creature's *power* and *toughness*. A creature's power indicates how much damage it does; normally, the Sprites would do 1 point of damage when they attack, but the Holy Strength enchantment says that the creature on which it is cast gains +1/+2, so your Sprites with Holy Strength now act as a 2/3 creature. They thus do 2 points of damage, and have a current toughness of 3.

You could attack with the Sprites now, but you decide to save them for defense. If you attack, the Sprites will become tapped, and if they're tapped, they can't defend.

The main phase of a turn—the part we just saw—includes casting spells, a single attack that may involve any or all of your creatures on the table, and playing a single land card. These things can happen in any order. The last part of a turn, the discard phase, occurs only if you have more than seven cards in your hand; it forces you to discard until you have seven. Right now you have less than that, so you can't discard. You indicate your turn is over.

Now it's your opponent's turn. She untaps her lands, draws a card, and gets a really frustrated look on her face. Though she spends a while looking back and forth between her Drudge Skeletons and your Sprites, she decides not to actually do anything this turn.

Your turn. You draw a card, and, since it's another plains card, you lay it down on the table. Now you have two plains and one forest. You could cast Healing Salve, an *instant* that either gives you 3 life points or prevents up to 3 points of damage from being dealt to a creature, but you decide to save this until your need is greater. Besides, now you've got enough to summon a Pearled Unicorn, which costs 1 white mana and 2 of any color. You tap all your lands and put the Unicorn, a 2/2 creature, onto the table, savoring the dismayed look of your opponent.

Though you can't attack with the Unicorn this turn, you will be able to use it to defend, so you can attack with your Sprites and still not have to worry about her Skeletons. You announce an attack and tap the Sprites. Your opponent can't block with the Skeletons because your Sprites have the special ability *flying*. Only other flying creatures can block them, and the Skeletons don't fly. The Sprites thus wing merrily over to your opponent and prick her for 2 points of damage. You smile as you tell your opponent you're done.

Your opponent doesn't need to untap, since none of her cards became tapped since her last turn. She draws a forest card and plays it immediately. Then she announces that she is attacking and taps her Skeletons. This seems suspicious. Since the Skeletons are only 1/1 and your Unicorn is 2/2, the Skeletons will be killed if you block with your Unicorn. This isn't as bad for your opponent as it sounds, since the text block on the Skeletons card indicates it has a special ability called *regeneration*. Even if the Skeletons take enough damage to kill them, your adversary can spend 1 point of black mana to activate the regeneration ability and prevent them from dying. But her attack still seems pointless, since the Skeletons can do only 1 point of damage to your Unicorn, and the Unicorn won't be killed unless it takes damage equal to or greater than its toughness, which is 2. Your opponent may have made a mistake—or she may have something up her sleeve. Since you still have your Sprites, you decide to risk the Unicorn. You indicate that you're blocking.

Now you see what her sleeve held. She taps her forest, frees 1 point of green mana, and uses it to cast Giant Growth on her Skeletons. Similar to Holy Strength, Giant Growth gives the creature on which it is cast +3/+3, but unlike the Holy Strength bonus, this bonus lasts only until the end of the turn. Another difference between Holy Strength and Giant Growth is that Giant Growth is an *instant spell*, which means that it can be cast during an attack. Instants, along with *interrupt spells*, creature *special abilities* like regeneration, and the effects of some artifacts and enchantments, are called *fast effects*. Other types of spells, including *summons*, *enchantments*, *artifacts*, and *sorceries*, cannot be cast during an attack. Fast effects can also be cast during your opponent's turn, while you can cast other types of spells only during your own turn.

With that Giant Growth on them, the 1/1 Skeletons become 4/4 for this turn. They do 4 points of damage to the Unicorn, which has only 2 points of toughness. Since it has taken damage equal to or greater than its toughness, the Unicorn has taken enough damage to kill it. In return, it has done 2 points of damage, but the Skeletons now have a total of 4 points of toughness, so the Skeletons survive.

Now you wish you hadn't tapped all your mana, because that Healing Salve spell would be quite useful right here. Most creatures that take a lethal amount of damage go to the *graveyard*, otherwise known as the discard pile. If you could cast the Healing Salve, you could prevent 3 points of damage to your Unicorn. This would reduce the damage the Unicorn took from 4 points to 1, which wouldn't be enough to kill it. But you don't have any mana left, so the Unicorn goes to the graveyard and it's your opponent's turn to smile. Still, you've got your Sprites, and after all, you've got more life points!

Now that you've had this taste of the game, you can try a couple of different approaches. If you learn best by reading, go on and read the rest of the rulebook, then try a game with someone. If you learn better by doing, go ahead and play a game or two with somebody, and refer to the appropriate section of the rules if you get stuck. Then you can come back and read the whole book. Just be sure you do come back; if you don't, sooner or later some smart-aleck is going to catch you with a rule you won't know.

> *To help you get the most out of the Pocket Players'*
> *Guide, we've asked Selene the Sorceress and Mathias*
> *the Magician to add their explanations and comments*
> *to this version of the rules.*

 *Selene says: Hi, I'm Selene!*

 *Mathias says: Hi there. I'm Mathias.*

## At the Start of the Game

Each player must have at least forty cards in his or her deck.

 *Selene says: If you have enough cards, you may want to*
*construct several different decks designed around vari-*
*ous themes. I like to use a tight, 40-card "killer" deck for*
*tournaments, and larger "fun" decks for friendly play.*

*Mathias says: I like playing with two-color decks; using 60–70 cards seems to work best. One-color decks are more efficient, since you always have the right color of mana for your spells, but they are vulnerable if your opponent has a defense against that color. They tend to be more boring to play, too.*

Shuffle your deck thoroughly and wait for your opponent to do the same. You may request to shuffle your opponent's deck as well. Each of you then cuts the other person's deck and turns over the top card. These two cards are set aside as the ante. Whoever wins the game gets to keep both cards.

 *Mathias says: You may not want to play for ante, especially when you're first learning the game. That's fine too, as long as you and your opponent agree to this ahead of time. But you should still set the top card of each deck aside as a sort of "ghost" ante. That way your "ante" card will still be out of play for this game, but you get to keep it no matter who wins.*

Now draw seven cards from the top of your deck to form your starting hand. If you've just started playing, randomly select who goes first. Otherwise, the loser of the previous game goes first.

The space in front of you should now have a stack of undrawn cards, called the *library*; a space for your discards, known as the *graveyard*; and an area for you to place cards in play, called your *territory*. You may end up playing some cards in your opponent's territory. If you do, be sure to retrieve them at the end of the game. You might want to mark such cards with sticky notes or paper clips to make sure you remember to whom they belong.

*Selene says: When I play a card in Mathias's territory, I stick a plastic card holder—available at trading card stores—on it. That way he doesn't accidentally stick it back in his own deck at the end of the game.*

## Game Turn

During his or her turn, each player must perform the following steps, also called *phases*:

1. Untap.
2. Upkeep.
3. Draw a card.
4. Main Phase (in any order):
    a. May put a land into play.
    b. May make an attack.
    c. May cast spells.
5. Discard down to seven cards in hand, if necessary.
6. Inform opponent you are finished.
7. Heal creatures.

Strictly speaking, you need to give your opponent a chance to act after every part of this sequence, and even after every action you take. Most games are far more informal, and you can expect your adversary to jump in with a "Wait!" before you go on.

## Tapping and Untapping

Many cards have the following symbol on them: 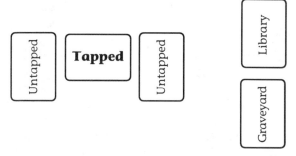. If a card has this symbol, the card must be tapped whenever its power or ability is used; this indicates it cannot be used again until untapped. Tapping a card means turning it horizontally. At the beginning of your turn, you untap all of your cards. This initial untapping of cards occurs instantaneously, which means that neither you nor your opponent can play spells or fast effects before or during your untap phase.

*Selene says: Untapping your cards during the untap phase isn't optional; it's required unless a card prevents you from untapping something or says you don't have to. If you forget to untap something, it's usually no big deal; just do it when you notice.*

## Upkeep

Some cards require you to take some action during your upkeep. This requirement will be stated specifically on the cards. If you don't have any such cards in play, move directly to the draw phase. You or an opponent may also play fast effects during this phase.

 *Mathias says: The upkeep phase is the first opportunity during your turn for you to cast spells or use creature abilities, since the untap phase happens all at once and ends immediately.*

 *Selene says: Even if you don't have any cards that require upkeep, the upkeep phase still happens. I like to cast my Mana Short during Mathias's upkeep phase; it taps all his lands and drains his mana, so casting it during his upkeep pretty much keeps him from doing anything useful that turn. Also, keep in mind that you can cast an enchantment to make a card require extra upkeep even if it didn't require upkeep originally.*

## Draw

This phase is pretty simple. Draw a card from the top of your library and put it in your hand. If you have no cards in your library when you need to draw, the game ends and your opponent wins. Only fast effects may be used during this phase; other spells have to wait until the Main Phase.

 *Mathias says: I once won a duel by casting a spell to make Selene draw ten cards when she only had nine left in her library. Even though I cast the spell on my turn rather than during her draw phase, she still lost when she couldn't draw enough cards.*

## Main Phase

This phase is a little trickier. You may play a land card from your hand if you want to, but you may not play more than one. You may have some or all of your creatures in play attack your opponent, but you can't change your mind about who's attacking and who isn't once your opponent has begun to declare defense. You cannot attack more than once per turn. You may play the land card either before or after the attack. This is the only phase during which you may cast summons, enchantments, sorceries, or artifacts. You may cast these spells any time during this phase except during an attack.

 *Selene says: I usually play the land first so I don't forget, then cast spells, and then attack. But sometimes I wait to cast spells until after attacking. I faked Mathias out, once: I didn't play a land, used all my mana, and then attacked. He thought I couldn't do anything more to him, so he used all his mana defending against my attack. When the attack was over, I put down a mountain, tapped it, and shot him with a Lightning Bolt.*

 *Mathias says: Yeah, you can get tricky. But remember, you can't play land during the attack, only before or after. And you only get to attack once during your turn, even if you have some untapped creatures available after the attack.*

## Discard

If you have more than seven cards, you have to discard enough cards to bring your hand down to seven. If you have seven cards or fewer, you may not discard. As with the Draw phase, only fast effects may be used during this phase.

## Inform Opponent

Because you may not need to discard and there's no set order to the main phase, your adversary has no way of knowing you're finished with your turn unless you announce it.

*Selene says: We got in the habit of knocking on the table and saying "Done" at the end of the turn. Now I keep doing it while playing chess, and everyone looks at me strangely.*

*Mathias says: At this point in your opponent's turn, you get one last chance to use those fast effects you've been saving. This is when Selene likes to hit me with her Prodigal Sorcerer's direct damage ability, if she hasn't already used it to shoot one of my creatures. Sometimes she forgets she saved it and starts her own turn. I say that's tough luck, the price she pays for trying to be too sneaky.*

## Heal Creatures

Once you say you're done, your opponent can, as usual, respond with fast effects, to which you may respond. When all this is finished, any damage to creatures in play is erased. Now it's your opponent's turn.

*Selene says: By the way, this part of the turn, after erasing the damage, is when spells and special abilities that apply "until end of turn" go away, when creatures like the Scavenging Ghoul that get counters at the end of the turn get them, and when creatures die if a spell or effect forces them to die "at end of turn."*

# Winning the Game

Each player starts the game with 20 life points. If your opponent's life point total drops below 1 at the end of a phase or at the start or end of an attack, you win. If both players reach or go below 0 at one of these times, the game is a draw. You also win if your opponent is required to draw a card but has no cards left in his or her library.

> *Mathias says: Notice that you can go below 1 during a phase and still survive, if you heal yourself before the end of the phase.*

# Mana

Most spells require mana to cast. Mana can be one of five colors—white, blue, black, red, or green—or it can be colorless. Some spells will require a certain amount of a particular type of mana, while others can be cast with any type.

## Sources of Mana

The most common source of mana are land cards. Different kinds of land provide different colors of mana (see the Mana Chart for more information). A land card can usually provide only one point of mana per turn. If you draw mana from a land card, you must tap it to show that the mana has been drawn from it.

> *Selene says: If you have a way to untap a land card in the middle of a turn, you can tap it again and get another point of mana from it. Also, your opponent*

*may try to use a spell to tap your land and keep you
from drawing mana from it, but this doesn't quite
work. We'll explain why later on.*

The five basic land types are plains, which produce white
mana; mountains, which produce red mana; forests, which
produce green mana; swamps, which produce black mana;
and islands, which produce blue mana. Basic lands have no
other abilities. Some effects in the game may change a land
into any one of the basic land types. If this happens, the

---

### Mana Chart

**Black Magic:** The black magician's power stems from
the swamps and bogs. Black magic is the magic of death.
The often self-destructive lore of black magic is regarded
by most as best left unknown. The traditional enemies of
black are white and green.

**Blue Magic:** The blue magician taps the islands for
energy. Blue magic is mental in nature. The fortes of the
blue magician are artifice, illusion, and deception, as well as
the elemental forces of air and water. The traditional enemies of blue are red and green.

**Green Magic:** The green magician draws energy from
the forest. Many magicians have been lulled into complacency
by green magic's peaceful exterior, the magic of life, and have
been caught unaware by the vast destructive capability of its
nature. Green's traditional enemies are blue and black.

**Red Magic:** The red magician gets power from the mountains. Red magic is a destructive magic, the magic of earth and
of fire, of chaos and of war. The traditional enemies of red are
blue and white.

**White Magic:** The white magician draws energy from
the plains. Spells of healing and protection are the white
magician's specialty, though chivalrous war magic is not
unfamiliar. White's traditional enemies are red and black.

land loses any special powers it might have had, and the kind of mana it produces may change.

Mana can also come from various other sources in the game; these are all explained on the relevant cards.

 *Mathias says: That's why the rules talk about "green" mana instead of "forest" mana, and so forth; it's not just to make things more confusing, it's because lands aren't the only mana sources.*

## Mana Pool

When you draw mana from any source, such as a land, it goes into your *mana pool*. Your mana pool is simply the mana you have available at that moment. When you cast a spell, the mana you use is drawn from your mana pool. If for some reason there is mana left in your mana pool at the end of any phase or at the beginning or end of an attack, each remaining point of mana is converted into a point of damage to you. The source of this damage is considered colorless.

 *Selene says: Are you confused? This part puzzles a lot of people, who wonder, "Why would I ever have mana left? Don't I just tap land at the time I'm casting the spell, and tap only as much as I need?" Well, ninety-nine percent of the time, that's true. It's just that there are a few spells and effects that make you get more than 1 mana at a time. For example, you might have a forest with the spell Wild Growth on it. Tapping this forest will give you 🌳 🌳 . If the spell you're casting only costs 🌳 then you need to either find a way to use*

*up the other* , *or take 1 point of colorless damage from the leftover mana.*

You may not give mana to another player. Tapping a land to add mana to your mana pool is considered an interrupt.

*Mathias says: That last sentence is important, even though we haven't gotten around to talking about what interrupts are yet. You can skip ahead to Interrupts and Interrupts and Timing if you get impatient.*

## Parts of a Magic Card

If the spell is a Summon spell, the card will indicate what class of creature is being summoned. For example, Wall of Wood, Wall of Bone, and Wall of Swords all say "Summon Wall," which is important if there's another spell that kills all walls.

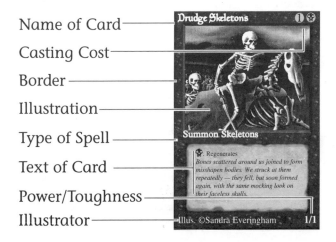

- Name of Card
- Casting Cost
- Border
- Illustration
- Type of Spell
- Text of Card
- Power/Toughness
- Illustrator

*Selene says: That class is the only part of the card you should look at when trying to decide if a spell affects a particular card. If a spell affects "all Zombies," it only works on cards that say "Summon Zombie," no matter what the picture or the other text on the card may imply.*

Power and toughness appear only on creature cards. See **The Attack** for more information.

## Spells and Permanents

There are six basic kinds of spells: summons, enchantments, sorceries, instants, interrupts, and artifacts. When you play any card that's not a land, you are casting a spell. Once a card is successfully played, it is no longer a spell. Some spells are discarded after being cast; others, called *permanents*, remain in play. Lands, artifacts, creatures, and enchantments are all permanents once they are in play. Sometimes tokens can represent permanents (see **Tokens and Counters** for more information). Almost all permanents are played in the caster's territory. The exception is enchantments that say "Enchant *something*," where *something* is another type of card, such as a creature. These *enchant card* spells are played on their targets.

*Selene says: Note that you can never play an enchantment on your opponent. Enchantments that aren't enchant card spells always go in your own territory, and if they say "you" it means just you, not your opponent.*

The caster of a card is usually considered its *controller*, though some effects can change this. If a card refers to "you" or "your," then it means the current controller of that card. If an effect gives control of a card to someone other than the caster, place the card in the territory of its new controller. Make sure you retrieve your cards from your opponent's territory after a game!

> *Mathias says: It really is a good idea to stick something on your cards so your opponent doesn't accidentally walk away with them after the game. I found a black Paralyze card in my red-and-green deck after one tournament, and couldn't remember who it belonged to.*

Once a permanent is in play, only the effects of another card can remove it. In other words, you can't just decide you want it to go away, even if it's yours.

> *Selene says: Mathias once cast Weakness on one of my creatures. I had three Power Leaks in my hand, and cast them all on his Weakness enchantment! Those three Power Leaks would have cost him* **6** *or 6 life-points during each of his upkeeps, so he had to use his only Disenchant spell to destroy his Weakness and get rid of them.*

## Tokens and Counters

Some cards will tell you to use tokens or counters. Usually, these counters are merely memory aids placed on a card; for example, a +1/+1 counter may be placed on a creature to help you remember that its power and toughness have increased. A memory-aid counter cannot be the target of any spell or effect.

Occasionally, however, a card will ask you to use a token to represent a permanent, such as a creature. These tokens are considered permanents and are affected by spells and effects that affect the appropriate type of permanent, but they are not considered cards. If any effect causes a token to leave play, remove it from the game altogether; tokens cannot be sent to the graveyard, returned to their owners' hands, or otherwise maintained out of play.

## Casting Cost

The cost to cast a spell is listed in the upper right-hand corner of the card. It will consist of one or more numbers in gray circles and/or mana symbols. The symbols indicate how much mana of a particular type is needed to cast the spell, and the gray-circled numbers indicate how much more mana of any combination of types is needed. For example, ③ ✹ ✹ would be listed on a spell that takes 2 white mana and 3 more of any type to cast. The 3 mana of any type could be 2 green and 1 blue, 3 more white, or 2 colorless mana and 1 black, for example.

Some spells may have an X in the gray circle. Unless otherwise specified on the card, this means that the caster may use any amount of mana available to fulfill that part of the casting cost, even 0. The text on such cards explains what the effect of this X mana will be. For example, Disintegrate has a casting cost of Ⓧ ⏣ , and the text says "Disintegrate does X damage to one target." If the caster spends 1 red mana plus 4 more of any type, Disintegrate would do 4 points of damage.

 *Mathias says: Why would you ever want to cast an X spell with X = 0? Usually you wouldn't, but sometimes it can be useful. Remember that bit about taking damage if you have leftover mana in your mana pool? If you had an extra* 🌑 *, you could cast a 0-point Disintegrate to get rid of it. Or you could imitate one of my more clever opponents: cast a 0-point Disintegrate on a regenerating creature, and then use another card to kill it. Since Disintegrate also says "If target dies this turn, target is removed from the game entirely," the Disintegrate will keep the creature from regenerating even though some other card actually killed it. Pretty sneaky!*

When a card refers to the casting cost of a spell, it means the total number of mana needed, ignoring how much is of what type. A spell that requires 1 💀 💀 to cast thus has a casting cost of 3. If a card refers to the casting cost of a spell that is not currently being cast, assume X is 0. Tokens representing permanents are also assumed to have a 0 casting cost.

## Targets

Some spells or effects require one or more targets. This sort of spell or effect allows the caster to choose which of a particular class of cards will be affected. Usually the type of target will be obvious; for instance, an *enchant land* spell can only be cast on a land. A spell that requires a target may not be cast if there are no targets of the appropriate type available. For example, you can't cast an *enchant creature* spell unless there's a creature on the table, and you can't power an enchantment that protects you from a source of blue magic unless you're taking damage from a blue card. An effect which occurs when a creature blocks or is blocked by something is not considered targeted.

*Mathias says: This rule prevents players from circumventing the rule about taking damage from unspent mana. You can't pump all the excess mana into some targetless spell or effect just to avoid the damage.*

Some spells or effects act on an entire class of cards; for example, a card might destroy all creatures in play. This sort of spell doesn't give the caster any choice about which of the cards in the class will be affected, so it does not have a specific target. Cards affected by such a spell are not considered targets, and such spells may be cast whether or not there is a card of the appropriate class in play.

*Selene says: If the spell is a vanilla enchantment (as opposed to an enchant card enchantment), it sticks around even if there's nothing for it to affect. For example, Mathias has Bad Moon, an enchantment that gives +1/+1 to all black creatures in play. He can cast this even if there are no black creatures out yet; it stays there, ready to help any black creatures that get played later. You can think of it as enchanting the table, rather than enchanting a specific card.*

If a spell conceals the identity of a card, you may target that card as long as the available information indicates that card *could* be a legitimate target. For example, if a spell conceals the identity of a creature, you may target that card with an effect that destroys walls, even though you can't be sure it's a wall. If the concealed card doesn't turn out to be a valid target, the targeting spell is discarded with no effect.

If you have a spell that targets a permanent, you may not use your spell on your opponent's permanent until it has been successfully brought into play. Until then, your opponent's permanent is just a spell, subject only to effects that target spells.

*Mathias says: Say, for example, that Selene is casting a spell to bring out her Rod of Ruin. I have a Shatter in my hand, which can destroy any Artifact. I can't cast Shatter until the Rod of Ruin is in play, since before that, it's just a spell. So, she'll get to zap me with it at least once, whatever I do. Or, suppose I cast Weakness (a −2/−1 enchant creature spell) on her Benalish Hero (1/1). She has a Disenchant in her hand, which can destroy any enchantment, but she can't use it to save the Hero because by the time the Weakness becomes a legal target, the Hero is already on the way to the graveyard. (Note: Some spells refer to cards "in play" as a shorthand way of saying "that have been successfully brought into play.")*

*Selene says: This also applies to your own spells. If I'm casting a Summon Pegasus, Mathias can interrupt it with a Spell Blast, countering my spell. I can't cast Death Ward to save the Pegasus, since Death Ward only affects creatures, and the Summon Pegasus spell doesn't become a creature until it is successfully cast.*

## Sacrificing

If a card calls for a *sacrifice*, you must choose an appropriate card in play and place it in your graveyard. This card is considered *buried* and thus may not be regenerated (see **Destroyed, Buried, and Removed from Game**). You cannot sacrifice a card under another player's control or a card that is already leaving play.

*Selene says: You can't sacrifice a card that is not in play or that is leaving play, so you can't sacrifice a creature that has already taken lethal damage unless you regenerate it first, and you can't sacrifice a creature that has been Unsummoned. Though you can't sacrifice a card that's not under your control, you can sacrifice another player's card if you can get control of it first. Finally, though you can't regenerate sacrificed creatures in any way—including the use of Death Ward—you can retrieve them from death with Raise Dead, just like any other creature in your graveyard.*

A sacrifice is a cost that cannot be prevented. Any effects that would normally prevent a card from being destroyed or damaged do not protect the card from being sacrificed. Also, just as mana is spent as soon as a spell is announced, a sacrifice is taken as soon as the spell or effect requiring it is announced. If this spell or effect is countered in some way, the card being sacrificed still gets buried, just as the mana spent on a countered spell is still spent.

*Mathias says: This means if Selene casts Sacrifice and I counter it with a Spell Blast, the creature she had to sacrifice has already gone to her graveyard and must stay there; she just doesn't get any benefit from it.*

*Selene says: Note that sacrificing something is not the same as destroying it. A card that says it cannot be destroyed, can still be sacrificed. Also, you can sacrifice a card with protection from black (see **Protection** under **More on Special Abilities**) even if the card requiring the sacrifice is black. Sacrificing a card is a distinct action you take as a player to meet the requirements of*

*another card; it's treated differently from destroying,
burying, and other effects that remove cards from play.*

## Additional Costs

Some permanents have special effects or abilities that can
be activated after the cards are in play. These costs will
appear in the text block, and are called *activation costs*.
See **Artifacts**, **Creature Abilities**, and **Enchantments** for
more information.

## Artifacts

*Mathias says: Bringing an artifact into play is the same
as casting any spell; it can be countered by an interrupt. Once it's been successfully cast, it can only be
affected by spells that affect artifacts.*

You may cast artifacts only during your main phase. All
artifacts except artifact creatures may be used during the
turn in which they are played. If an artifact becomes tapped
you may not use it again until it is untapped, even if it does
not normally tap. Even continuous effects of the artifact
cease until it is untapped.

*Selene says: How would an artifact with continuous
effects ever get tapped? Well, some spells may allow
you to tap it, like the First Edition spell Twiddle. This
can be very effective. For example, Mathias has the
artifact Library of Leng, which allows him to keep any
number of cards in his hand. If I use Twiddle to tap it
during his turn, he has to discard all but seven cards at
the end of his turn. Another example: I have the artifact Winter Orb, which prevents players' lands from
untapping normally during the untap phase. If I use*

*Twiddle to tap it at the end of Mathias's turn, it will be tapped at the beginning of my untap phase, so it can't generate any effects. Thus, I can untap all my land and the Orb in my own untap phase. So when Mathias's turn rolls around, the Orb will be untapped, preventing Mathias from untapping when his next turn rolls around.*

Artifacts often have a cost to use, which is listed in the text area of the card. If an artifact shows a  symbol in the text block, you must tap the artifact whenever you use it. If there are mana symbols next to an artifact's effect, then you must provide that mana to use that effect. If there is neither a tap symbol nor any other cost to activate, the artifact is continuous and its effect is always present unless the artifact becomes tapped. An artifact with an activation cost of **0** is not continuous; it is activated only when its controller announces he or she is activating it.

*Mathias says: That's a lot to chew on there, so let us give you a few examples. Glasses of Urza: ⟨tap⟩. Tapping these lets you see your opponent's hand. You can use these once, and then they stay tapped until your next untap phase.*

*Selene says: Rod of Ruin: ⟨tap⟩ **3**. Spend 3 mana and ⟨tap⟩ tap the card to do a point of damage. Again, it stays tapped until your next untap phase.*

*Mathias says: Throne of Bone: **1**. This one has no symbol, so it can be used multiple times per turn. Each time a black spell is cast, you can spend 1 mana of any color and gain 1 life.*

*Selene says: Library of Leng: This one has no  and no mana cost, so it just keeps working all the time, unless it gets tapped by something else.*

 *Mathias says: Remember, if an artifact requires a particular event to occur before you can use it—like Throne of Bone— you can only use the artifact once per event. You can't pump* **9** *through the Throne unless nine separate black spells have been cast. If you have two Thrones, though, you can spend* **1** *on each of them and get 2 life points per black spell cast. The cost must still be paid individually for each artifact.*

## Artifact Creatures

Artifact creatures are artifacts that must also follow the restrictions on creatures. Thus they may not attack or use any ability whose cost includes the  symbol on the turn they are summoned, and they may not attack or defend when tapped. Artifact creatures can be targeted by spells that affect either artifacts or creatures (for more information, see **Creatures**).

 *Selene says: Mathias has an artifact creature called the Juggernaut, with a toughness of 3. Last game I zapped it with a Lightning Bolt, a spell that affects creatures; two games before that, I destroyed it with Shatter, a spell that affects artifacts. Artifact creatures are doubly vulnerable. But they are usually easier to summon than similar normal creatures would be.*

## Enchantments

Enchantments have a lasting effect on the game and may only be played during the main phase of the caster's turn.

Enchantments cannot be tapped; some enchantments are played on cards that can be tapped, but these enchantments function even when the target card is tapped. Enchantments that say "Enchant *something*," where *something* is another type of card, must be played on a card of the appropriate type. If the target of an *enchant card* enchantment ceases to be a legitimate target of the enchantment, the enchantment is discarded.

*Mathias says: I like casting Unholy Strength on my Skeletons—turns a wimpy 1/1 creature into a 3/2. Even more fun is piling several Unholy Strength spells onto one Skeleton.*

*Selene says: Well, I like casting Power Leak on his Unholy Strength enchantments. Spells that say "Enchant Enchantment" can be cast on any enchantment or enchant card card. You can even cast Power Leak on your opponent's Power Leak! When you have a pile of enchantments affecting each other like this, a single Disenchant on the first enchantment will send all of them to their owners' graveyards.*

If the card just says it's an enchantment, place it in the caster's territory. Such enchantments affect both players unless the card says otherwise.

*Mathias says: The Bad Moon card that Selene mentioned earlier is this type of enchantment. Selene doesn't usually play with black, so it's a good card for me to use when I'm playing against her, but when I'm playing other people I have to be careful that it doesn't help them more than it helps me!*

*Selene says: On the other hand, I have a card called Orcish Oriflamme, which gives a +1/+0 to all of my creatures when they're attacking. That enchantment says "your," so it only affects*

> *my creatures, not my opponent's. Any "you" on an enchant-
> ment card always means the enchantment's controller, and
> "your" always means cards you control, not cards you own.*

Some enchantments have activation costs. This cost may only
be paid by the controller of the enchantment. Such enchantments may be used more than once per turn, and may even be
used more than once at a time. For example, if you play a
creature enchantment that adds 1 to the target creature's
power for each ![symbol], you can spend ![symbol] ![symbol] ![symbol] to add 3 to
the creature's power. These may be spent all at once or one at
a time—simultaneously or sequentially. All such activated
power and toughness bonuses expire at the end of the turn.

*Mathias says: If you cast an enchantment on one of your
opponent's cards, you are still the controller of that enchantment. You are the only one who can spend mana on its
activation cost or upkeep. If you cast an enchantment on
one of your own creatures and your opponent later takes
control of the creature, you still control the enchantment.*

*Selene says: Circles of Protection are the most com-
mon enchantment with an activation cost. You can
use a Circle as many times per turn as you have mana
to spend on it and damage to target. Say I have a
Circle of Protection: Black and Mathias attacks me
with a Skeleton and two Zombies. I spend* **3** *and
take no damage.*

## Sorceries

A sorcery may only be played during the caster's main
phase, and is discarded after use.

*Mathias says: Many spells that affect your opponent directly are sorceries—but not all! Remember that sorceries cannot be played during your attack phase, only before or after it.*

## Summons

A summon spell brings a creature into play. Creatures may only be summoned during the caster's main phase, and a creature of yours may not attack or use any ability whose activation cost includes the  symbol until it has been on your side from the very beginning of your turn.

*Selene says: This means my Prodigal Sorcerers can't shoot Mathias until the turn after I summon them. Oh well. Remember, special abilities that don't require tapping take effect the moment the creature is successfully summoned. And special abilities with no ⟁ symbol in the cost, such as regeneration (see **Regeneration** under **More on Special Abilities**), can be used during the turn the creature is summoned, even if they tap the creature.*

## Instants

An instant spell can be played during your turn or your opponent's turn. Instants are discarded once played. You may respond to a spell or other action with an instant and/or other fast effects, and your opponent may respond likewise until all fast effects are cast, at which time the instants all take effect, last to first (see **Timing** for more information).

*Mathias says: Instants can be played during the attack phase, too. This can get rather complex. We'll give some examples when they start talking about attacks.*

## Interrupts

An interrupt spell can be played during your turn or your opponent's turn. Though an interrupt is discarded once played, the effect it has on another spell is permanent. If you aren't sure you want to interrupt your opponent's spell, request some time to think. Once you or your opponent has taken any game action other than casting an interrupt, it is too late to interrupt a spell being cast. You may interrupt your own spells, and you and your opponent may cast more than one interrupt at a time. You may also interrupt an interrupt (see **Timing** for more information).

*Selene says: Here's an example that came up the other day. I cast a summon spell to bring up my favorite Prodigal Sorcerer, tapping an island and two mountains for the* 2 *cost.*

*Mathias says: I said "Wait," thought a moment, and pulled out a Spell Blast, tapping two islands and two swamps since Spell Blast costs* *plus the cost of the spell being cancelled. So much for that Sorcerer!*

*Selene says: But Mathias didn't know that I had a Spell Blast in my own hand. I happened to have four islands and a mountain left, which was just enough to Spell Blast his Spell Blast! He had no further counters so my Sorcerer made it through the exchange unscathed.*

*Mathias says: Oh well, I killed it a few turns later. Anyway, that's how interrupts work. Before going on to the next section, do note that second sentence: the effects of interrupts are permanent. This includes interrupts that change the color or text of a card. If, for example, I use an interrupt to change a Sea Serpent so that it swims through mountains instead of islands, this change is permanent.*

## Fast Effects

Fast effects include interrupts, instants, and the abilities of permanents. Some such abilities include regeneration, enhanced power and toughness, and providing mana. Most special abilities are described in the text block of the relevant card; you'll find descriptions of the others under **More on Special Abilities**. You may use fast effects at any time.

 *Selene says: The shooting ability of my Prodigal Sorcerer is an ability of a permanent, so it's a fast effect. In fact, any card power marked with 🅣 or a mana symbol is a fast effect. A bit further along we'll talk about the most common ones.*

## Creatures

Summon spells, mentioned earlier, bring creatures into play. You can easily identify creatures since they say "Summon *creature-type*" just below the illustrations and have two numbers separated by a slash in their lower right-hand corners. The spell cost in the upper right is the cost of the-summoning; once the card is on the table it is a creature, not a spell, and you do not have to pay the casting cost again.

## Power and Toughness

The two numbers in the lower right are the creature's *power* and *toughness*. The power rating indicates how much damage a creature does when it engages in combat. Toughness is how much damage the creature can take before it dies. This damage adds up during a turn, but is completely healed at the end of each turn unless the creature dies. If a creature's toughness drops below 1, it dies. If a creature's power drops below 1, it deals no damage when it engages in combat.

*Mathias says: It's important to remember that damage to creatures heals at the end of the turn, not the end of the attack. You can damage a creature in an attack, and then finish it off with a damage-dealing spell or fast effect later in the turn. That's why Selene likes to save her Prodigal Sorcerers for use late in the turn.*

*Selene says: Certain creatures base their power and toughness on the number of other cards in play. These show "\*/\*" in the lower right of the card, and the text explains how the values are determined. If one of these creatures is damaged but not killed, and later in the same turn one or more of the cards that determine its toughness are removed, the creature may die! Think of points of damage as invisible counters that you pile on the creature. If at any time the creature's toughness is less than or equal to the number of invisible damage counters on it, the creature falls over dead.*

*Mathias says: That may not be clear, so I'll give an example. I have a Keldon Warlord, whose special ability is that its power and toughness are equal to the number of my creatures in play. Along with the Warlord, I've got three Goblins, so the Warlord has a rating of 4/4. Selene attacks with her Grizzly Bears (2/2) and I block with the Warlord, who receives 2 points of damage. The Warlord is not a 4/2 creature now; it's a 4/4 creature with two points of damage. Later in the turn, Selene uses a Fireball to kill two of my Goblins. Since I now have two creatures in play, the Warlord becomes a 2/2 creature. It still has the 2 points of damage it took during the attack, so it goes to the graveyard.*

## Walls

Walls are just like other creatures except that they cannot be used to attack. Some walls have a power rating greater than zero; such a wall may be able to damage an attacker while defending, but it still cannot attack.

*Selene says: Since walls are creatures, you can cast enchant creature spells on them. Ever see a flying, Firebreathing wall? And they are also vulnerable to spells like Terror that destroy creatures. Yes, it's kind of silly to think of a wall being scared to death, but who ever said magic was logical?*

## Creature Characteristics

Some spells refer to the *characteristics* of a creature. These include the creature type, color, power, toughness, casting cost, and special abilities. They do not include any enchantments cast on the creature.

If a card refers to the power or toughness of a creature, this means its current power or toughness, including enchantments, unless the spell specifically says otherwise.

*Mathias says: For example, the Drain Life card says that if you use it on a creature, you can only gain as many life points as the creature has toughness. This means the creature's current toughness might be higher than the original toughness if it has an enchantment like Holy Armor on it, or lower if it has an enchantment like Weakness on it. Even if the creature has taken damage during the turn, you can still Drain Life on its whole toughness; damage doesn't subtract from toughness, it's just compared to toughness.*

## Special Abilities

Some creatures have special abilities, which are described in the text box. Using such an ability may require spending mana or tapping the creature; if so, the appropriate symbols will indicate this. If the activation cost for a special ability doesn't include the symbol, the ability may be used more than once per turn. Some creature abilities have activation costs that can be powered multiple times to generate greater effects. Such abilities add to the creature's natural abilities (see **More on Special Abilities** for more information).

*Selene says: My Prodigal Sorcerer's special shooting ability has the  symbol in its activation cost, so it can only be used once; I have to wait until I can untap it before I can use it again.*

*Mathias says: On the other hand, my Drudge Skeletons have the regeneration ability; its activation cost is 💀 , and doesn't include the 🌣 symbol. This means that it costs me 1 black mana each time they regenerate, but they can regenerate as many times per turn as they get killed—so long as I have the mana to pay for it. The regeneration taps them as a side effect, but it's not part of the cost.*

## "Summoning Sickness"

A creature of yours may not attack or use any ability whose activation cost includes the 🌣 symbol unless it was in play on your side at the start of your turn. This means most creatures can do nothing on the turn they are summoned, although they may block during your opponent's turn. This affliction is commonly refered to as summoning sickness.

*Selene says: Even if a creature has a special ability that lets it attack without being tapped, it still can't attack the turn it is brought into your territory. This applies whether it was summoned, returned from the grave, or even magically stolen from the other player's territory. Some cards allow you to break this rule, but they specifically say so. Remember, as I said before, special abilities that don't require tapping take effect the moment the creature is successfully summoned. For example, the Lord of Atlantis gives a bonus to all*

*Merfolk—even your opponent's—from the moment it hits the table, even though it can't attack that turn itself.*

 *Mathias says: And special abilities with a mana cost but no  symbol, like my Skeletons' regeneration, can be used during the turn they're summoned—which is a good thing, when Selene has that blasted Prodigal Sorcerer out.*

## The Attack

You may announce an attack only once per turn and only during your main phase. You select the attacking creatures, your opponent selects defenders, damage is dealt, and then the dead are carted away. During an attack, only fast effects may be played. No sorceries may be cast and no new enchantments, creatures, artifacts, or land may be put into play. Keep in mind that the following rules attempt to cover all cases and situations. Usually battles are pretty easy to follow.

 *Selene says: I like battles with creatures; I think that's where a lot of the fun and strategy comes in. Decks with no creatures may be effective, but they're just not as interesting to me.*

### Assigning Attackers

After you announce an attack, your opponent has the opportunity to respond with spells or special abilities that specify "before the attack." After these effects, if any, are resolved, you select any number of creatures under your control to participate in the attack, tapping them to indicate that they are being used to attack. Walls and creatures that were already tapped may not participate. After all attacking creatures have been chosen, either player may choose to use fast effects.

*Mathias says: After you've tapped your attackers, it's too late for your opponent to cast spells or use special abilities that have to be used before an attack. You have to give your opponent a chance to use them, though. I handle this by saying "I'm attacking" before I tap any of my attacking creatures. Selene can say "Wait," think about whether she wants to take any pre-attack actions, and then say "Go ahead." Then I pick the creatures with which I want to attack, tap them, and move them to a line in front of the rest of my cards, so Selene can easily assign defenders to them. Note that it is legal to declare an attack and then say you're attacking with no creatures! This uses up the attack phase and prevents the use of spells and abilities that must be cast before the attack.*

*Selene says: If I have an instant spell that can kill a creature, I often wait until after Mathias has declared which of his creatures are attacking. That way it's too late for him to add another creature to the attack.*

You cannot choose to attack your opponent's creatures. You can only push your army in the defender's general direction and see if your opponent chooses to block.

*Mathias says: This is one of the things that confuses new **Magic** players the most. You may want to attack a specific creature, but that's not allowed. Creatures*

*can only attack your opponent, and then it's his or her choice whether and how to block them. I often want to kill a particular creature of Selene's, like that Prodigal Sorcerer. But she refuses to attack or defend with it, so I'm out of luck unless I have a spell or effect that can kill it directly.*

## Assigning Defenders

Your opponent now chooses which creatures, if any, will defend. If any of your opponent's creatures are tapped, they may not defend. For each creature you have attacking, your opponent must decide how many, if any, creatures will block it. Your opponent may not use one creature to block two or more of yours, though more than one defender can block a single creature. Any attacking creature opposed by a defender is *blocked*, even if the defender is later removed by a fast effect or the block otherwise becomes illegal. After all defenders are assigned, there is another opportunity for fast effects.

*Selene says: Deciding how to defend can be tough, especially in a big battle with lots of creatures. Often I have to make tradeoffs, deciding whether it's better to kill Mathias's creature and lose my own as well, or lose a few life points but keep my creature and attack him with it later.*

*Mathias says: Notice that defending creatures are not tapped! This is another point that often confuses new* **Magic** *players. Just move the defending creature out in front of whichever attacker it's blocking. If the defender has a special ability that requires it to tap, and it survives the battle, you can still tap it for the special*

*ability afterwards. Does this give the defender an advantage? You bet!*

*Selene says: Pay particular attention to the rule that says the attacking creature is still blocked if the defender is removed by a fast effect. For example, say I'm attacking with a 1/1 Merfolk. Mathias has a 1/1 Goblin and decides to block the Merfolk with it. The Goblin will die, but it will kill the Merfolk and also keep them from doing a point of damage to him, so he thinks it's worth it. If I have an Unsummon spell, I could cast it on the Goblin now, sending the Goblin back into Mathias's hand. This would keep the Goblin from killing the Merfolk, but it would not let the Merfolk do a point of damage to Mathias; they were blocked, and they stay blocked. For the same reason, casting Jump on an attacker after it's been blocked won't let it fly past the blocker or even avoid damage. The only exception to this is if a spell specifically allows you to change blocking, like the First Edition False Orders spell.*

*Mathias says: This period—after defense but before damage dealing—is a good time to use fast effects that increase the strength of the creatures involved in the battle. Suppose I am attacking Selene with two Frozen Shades, creatures with the special ability*  *: +1/+1. I can wait until after she declares her defense before deciding how much mana to spend on each of the Shades. If she blocks one, I can put just enough strength into the blocked Shade to kill the defending creature, and most of my mana into the unblocked one.*

*Selene says: Of course, if he does that, I can respond with my own fast effects, like a Giant Growth spell. He could then add more mana to the Shade facing*

*my Giant-Growthed creature, if he had any left. The fast effects subphase continues until neither of us wants to use any more.*

## Damage

The next step is to assign damage. No spells or effects of any kind may be played while damage is being assigned. An unblocked attacker does an amount of damage equal to its power rating to your opponent. A blocked attacker does its damage to the defender blocking it; if the defender is no longer present, it does not deal damage at all. A defending creature deals damage to the attacker it blocked, unless it became tapped during the attack. Most defenders will remain untapped, but some may become tapped during the fast effects stage. All damage takes effect simultaneously.

 *Mathias says: How would a defender become tapped? Say Selene is attacking me, and I defend with Drudge Skeletons. She might have a spell she could cast, like Twiddle, to tap my card. Or she might cast a Lightning Bolt and kill them; I can spend 💀 to regenerate the Skeletons, but that leaves them tapped. In either of those cases, the Skeletons do no damage. In the regeneration case, the Skeletons don't take damage from the attacker either, because of special rules about regeneration (see **Regeneration** under **More on Special Abilities**). In all other cases with a tapped defender, the attacker still gets to damage the defender, but the defender doesn't hit back.*

 *Selene says: Another example: Suppose Mathias was attacking me, and I decided to block with my Prodigal Sorcerer. After declaring my defense, I could use the*

*Sorcerer's special ability as a fast effect, tapping it to do*
*a point of damage to Mathias or to another creature.*
*The creature my Sorcerer blocked is still blocked even*
*though the Sorcerer is tapped, but the Sorcerer will do*
*no damage to the creature it's blocking when damage-*
*dealing time rolls around.*

Next, compare the amount of damage a creature has taken
this turn to its toughness value. If the damage is equal to or
greater than its toughness, then the creature has taken a
lethal amount of damage. For example, if a creature with a
toughness of 6 took 2 points of damage from a spell earlier
in the turn and then was blocked by a creature with a power
of 4 during the attack, this creature sustained a total of 6
points of damage, enough to match its toughness and kill it.
If a creature takes more damage than its toughness rating,
that just makes it more thoroughly squashed. The extra
damage does not transfer to the defending player.

*Mathias says: The extra damage does make the creature*
*harder to save, though. Suppose I have a Grizzly Bear*
*(2/2) and a Samite Healer (1/1, 🪓 : prevent 1 point*
*of damage to any target). Selene attacks me with a*
*Hurloon Minotaur (2/3). I choose to block the*
*Minotaur with the Grizzly. The Grizzly now has 2*
*points of damage; since it has a toughness of 2, this will*
*kill it. But now I tap the Healer, preventing 1 point of*
*damage. This leaves the Grizzly with 1 point of dam-*
*age and 2 toughness, so it survives.*

*Now suppose instead of the Minotaur, Selene has a*
*Hill Giant (3/3). My Grizzly can still block, but the*
*Giant does 3 points of damage, so even if I tap my*
*Healer, the Grizzly is left with 2 points of damage and*
*2 toughness, so it dies. In both cases, though, only the*

> *creatures take damage; the block stops any damage
> from coming through to me. A 1/1 creature can block
> a 20/20 creature and take all twenty points of damage;
> this still doesn't damage the defending player.*

If two or more defending creatures block an attacking creature, the attacking player may assign damage from the attacker to the defenders as desired, even if this means one of the creatures takes more than enough damage to kill it.

> *Selene says: Take the same creatures Mathias just used
> in his example: I have a 3/3 Giant and he has a 2/2
> Grizzly and a 1/1 Healer. Since he knows that I can
> kill the Grizzly if he blocks only with it, he decides to
> block the giant with both creatures. Now I get to decide
> how to divide up the damage. I could do 3 points to the
> Grizzly and none to the Healer, 2 to the Grizzly and
> 1 to the Healer, 1 to the Grizzly and 2 to the Healer,
> or all 3 to the Healer. At first glance, the obvious
> choice would be 2 to the Grizzly and 1 to the Healer,
> killing both—but if I did that, he would tap the
> Healer, preventing a point of damage to whichever one
> he wanted to keep. So I should choose which one I
> really want to kill, and do all the damage to it.*

Once damage dealing starts, no other actions may occur until all damage has been assigned. After the damage is assigned, there is an opportunity to prevent the damage or redirect it; during this period, only damage prevention effects, damage redirection effects, regeneration effects, and interrupts may be used (see **Saving Creatures from the Grave** for more details).

> *Mathias says: Pay special attention to that sentence
> about what you can and can't do during the damage
> prevention/redirection period. You can't, for example,*

cast Unsummon to rescue a creature, or Giant Growth to make one tougher, since those are both instants, not interrupts. And you can't sacrifice a creature that has already taken lethal damage. Also, if a creature has a special ability that lets it gain strength or toughness from other creatures' deaths, this benefit does not take place until the victims actually go to the graveyard. Since this won't happen until after all damage prevention and redirection has taken place, the bonus the creature gains from the other creatures' deaths will not let it do more damage or survive an attack that would otherwise kill it.

## More on Special Abilities

Any special ability that includes the  symbol in the activation cost may not be used if the creature is already tapped. Abilities that do not include  in the activation cost may be used whether the creature is tapped or not.

 *Selene says: Note once again that regeneration can be used on tapped creatures, since tapping is a side effect of regeneration, not part of the activation cost.*

Creature special abilities that require neither tapping nor payment to use are always in effect. Note that this means creatures cannot choose *not* to use these abilities where applicable, though a creature with a special ability that gives it an advantage when attacking is not required to attack. For example, a creature with the special ability *flying* cannot choose to attack on foot, but you don't have to attack with that creature unless you want to. The one exception to this rule is *banding*; you may decide whether and how a creature with this ability chooses to band (see **Evasion Abilities** and **Banding** for more information on these abilities).

> *Mathias says: This means I can't let Selene block my flying creature with a non-flying creature, even if I've got some nifty spell that would do dastardly things to her blocker. Of course, I could always cast Jump on her creature, though that would probably make her pretty suspicious.*

## Enhanced Power/Toughness

One common special ability is enhanced power or toughness. For example, a creature may have the ability to gain 1 point of power for . If is spent, the creature's power is increased by 4. This ability can also be used again later in the turn, multiple times if needed. All such special ability bonuses expire at the end of the turn.

> *Selene says: Frozen Shades are the most common creature with this ability. They have a base rating of 0/1, but for every ☠ you spend, they gain +1/+1 until the end of the turn. Usually the best time to spend this mana is during the fast effects period after defense is declared but before damage is dealt. You can also use it when your opponent casts a spell to kill the creature. For example, if I shoot Mathias's Frozen Shade with my Prodigal Sorcerer for 1 point of damage, he can respond by spending ☠, raising it to 1/2 and thus keeping it alive.*

When the rules or cards refer to a creature's power or toughness, they mean the current value, which may have been increased or decreased from the original numbers in the lower right of the card as a result of special abilities, enchantments, or other effects.

*Mathias says: So if I had enough mana, I could put 5 black mana into the Frozen Shade, raising it to 5/6 for the rest of the turn. Then I could cast Drain Life on it and gain up to 5 life from it without killing it.*

## Regeneration

Usually, when a creature is about to be sent to the graveyard, it can be regenerated by an appropriate spell or ability. A regenerated creature returns to play tapped but undamaged, and never actually reaches the graveyard. A creature that is *buried* or *removed from the game* cannot be regenerated (see **Destroyed, Buried, and Removed from Game**).

*Selene says: After regenerating, the creature regains its full toughness, including any bonuses from fast effects earlier in the turn, and all damage it has taken is discarded. All enchantments on the creature stay there, and the creature is not considered killed or destroyed. The creature can still take damage and be killed again, if another spell affects it later in the turn.*

*Note that if the creature lost counters due to damage, these counters stay lost. If this leaves the creature at 0 toughness after regenerating, then it dies again immediately, unless you can increase its toughness with another fast effect!*

If a creature that has been declared as an attacker or blocker is regenerated before damage is dealt, that creature neither receives nor deals damage in that attack. However, if the regenerating creature was blocking an attacking creature, the attacking creature is still considered blocked.

*Mathias says: For example, the Basilisk has a special ability that says any creature that blocks it is destroyed. Let's say I use the Basilisk to block Selene's Hill Giant. Selene then casts two Lightning Bolts, which kill the Basilisk. But I cast Death Ward and regenerate the Basilisk. Though the Basilisk neither receives damage from the Hill Giant nor deals damage to it, its special ability still takes effect and destroys the Hill Giant.*

*Selene says: Another example: Some spells and effects can force a creature to attack or be destroyed. Let's say I use such an effect on one of Mathias's Skeletons. He attacks with it, and it is killed and regenerated before it's time to deal damage. Though it neither receives damage from nor deals damage to the creature blocking it, it did fulfill the need to attack, so it isn't destroyed.*

## Evasion Abilities

Some creatures have the *flying* ability, which means they can be blocked only by other flying creatures, though they can block both flying and nonflying creatures. Other creatures have *landwalk* abilities, such as swampwalk or forestwalk. If the defending player has a land of the appropriate type in play, such as a swamp for a swampwalking creature, then an attacking creature with that type of landwalk cannot be blocked, even by other creatures with the same ability.

*Selene says: We get a lot of questions about flyers vs. nonflyers, so let's go over this carefully. Say Mathias has a Scryb Sprites (flying) and a Shanodin Dryad (forest-walk). I have a Merfolk (no special abilities). If I attack him, he can block with either creature or with both of them. If he attacks me with the Scryb Sprites, I can't block because the Merfolk can't fly. He can't "let me block" even if he wants to kill the Merfolk. If he attacks with the Dryad and I have no forests, I can block normally. If I have any forests in play, then I can't block the Dryad, not even with a Dryad of my own.*

*Mathias says: Another example with the same creatures: I declare I'm attacking with both the Sprites and the Dryad. If Selene casts Jump on her Merfolk before declaring her defense, she can assign the Merfolk to block the Sprites since now they can fly too. But if she forgets about the Jump and says she isn't blocking, she can't change her mind later.*

*Now, let's say it's Selene's turn to attack. She still has her Merfolk, but she Terrorized my Sprites so now I have only my Dryad left. If she casts Jump on her Merfolk before I declare my defense, her Merfolk can bounce right over my Dryad. But if Selene has recently been, say, hit on the head, she could forget to cast the Jump until after I declare that my Dryad is blocking. In that case, her Jump would come too late; since my Dryad is already blocking the Merfolk, they can't get through even though they can now fly.*

## Trample

All damage delivered by a creature with the *trample* ability is considered *trample damage*. If a defending creature takes more trample damage than is needed to kill it, the excess trample damage is applied to the defending player. If the poor defending creature finds itself receiving both normal and trample damage, apply the normal damage first.

*Selene says: Suppose I have a War Mammoth (3/3, trample) and attack Mathias with it. He blocks with Drudge Skeletons (1/1, regenerates). The Skeletons take 3 points of trample damage. Only 1 point is needed to kill them, so Mathias suffers the other 2 points of trample damage and regenerates the Skeletons. Next turn, we're in the same situation, but this time the War Mammoth is banded (see **Banding** later in this section) with a Benalish Hero (1/1). In this case, the Skeletons take 1 point of normal damage from the Hero and 3 points of trample damage from the Mammoth. We apply the normal damage first, find that it's enough to kill the Skeletons, and deal all 3 points of trample damage to Mathias. Whether the Skeletons regenerate or not makes no difference to the damage Mathias takes.*

*Mathias says: If a creature with trample is blocked by two or more defenders, the attacking player can choose to assign all the trample damage to one defending creature; any excess trample damage then gets through to the defending player. The attacking player could also spread the trample damage around over several of the defenders, but if any defending creature takes more trample damage than is necessary to kill it, the excess will spill over onto the defending player. If the defenders are banded, then the defender chooses how to allocate the damage; still, any trample damage in excess of what it takes to kill the creatures to which it is assigned still spills over onto the player. If a blocking creature has protec-*

> *tion from the trampling creature's color (see **Protection** later in this section), then the defending player takes no damage, since the damage has to be applied to the creature first and the creature is immune to it.*

If a creature with the trample ability is considered blocked, but the creature blocking it is removed before damage is dealt, then all trample damage is applied to the player (see the **Example of Creature Combat** for more information).

*Selene says: Note that trample damage only occurs when a creature with trample is attacking, not when it's blocking! If Mathias attacks me with those Skeletons and I defend with the same War Mammoth, no excess damage spills over onto him. Another example: Let's say my Mammoth attacks Mathias and he chooses not to block, but he has some spell or effect that lets him redirect the damage from himself to his Skeletons. Once the damage has been redirected it is no longer considered trample damage, so the excess will not spill over onto Mathias.*

## First Strike

If a creature has *first strike*, it deals its damage first. Creatures receiving this damage must survive it before they can deal any return damage; if an opposing creature takes lethal damage from a creature with first strike, it cannot return the attack. During an attack, all creatures with first strike deal their damage simultaneously, then surviving creatures without first strike deal their damage simultaneously. Giving a creature the first strike ability twice does not allow it to deal damage before others with first strike.

*Mathias says: For example, let's say a White Knight (2/2, first strike) is blocked by a Gray Ogre (2/2, no special abilities). The Knight deals its damage first, doing 2 points of damage to the Ogre, which is enough to kill it. Unless something prevents this damage, the Ogre dies without doing its 2 points of damage to the Knight in return. Replace the Ogre with a Hurloon Minotaur (2/3), and the Knight no longer does enough damage to kill its opponent, so the Minotaur gets to strike back and kill the Knight.*

## Banding

Banding creatures have two powers, both of which can be used only during an attack phase.

When attacking, a banding creature may join with one or more other attacking creatures. These creatures must then be blocked or allowed through together. When you declare which creatures are attacking, you must also declare which attackers, if any, are banding and who they are banding with. If a defending creature can block any one of these creatures, it can block the entire group, even if it would not normally be able to block some of them individually. If the creatures are blocked, the damage they receive from the blocking creature or creatures is distributed among the attackers however the attacking player wishes. A banding creature may join with any number of other attacking creatures as long as no more than one of the creatures does *not* have the banding ability.

*Mathias says: Say I have a Mesa Pegasus (1/1, flying, banding) and a Bog Wraith (3/3, swampwalk). I band them together and attack Selene. If she has no*

swamps in play, then she can block both the Pegasus and the Wraith with her Hurloon Minotaur (2/3), since the Wraith can't use its swampwalk ability to sneak past, and banding requires the Pegasus to stay with the Wraith. If she has a swamp in play, she can't block the Wraith; now the only way she can block the banded creatures is if she has a flying creature that can block the Pegasus. Let's say she does have a Pegasus of her own, and blocks my Pegasus with it. Since my Wraith and Pegasus are banded, I get to decide where the point of damage from her Pegasus goes; naturally, I assign it to the Bog Wraith, who is tough enough not to die from it. If my attacking creatures hadn't been banded, her Pegasus would have blocked mine, killing them both, but my Bog Wraith would have swamp-walked on through.

Selene says: Banding only helps when distributing damage to or from blocking creatures. Damage from spells and effects cannot be diverted by banding; if I had used a Lightning Bolt to zap Mathias's Bog Wraith in the example above, he would not have been able to assign that damage to the Pegasus instead. Damage to the defending player from banded attacking creatures is treated exactly as if the creatures had attacked individually. For example, you must power the appropriate Circles of Protection once per creature, not just once versus the whole band.

When defending, any creature can join with one or more other creatures to block a single attacker; the attacker's damage is then distributed among the blockers as the attacking player sees fit. But if any *one* of the blocking creatures has the banding ability, then damage from the attacking creatures is distributed among the blockers as the *defending* player desires. The defending player may assign more damage to a creature than it can survive.

> *Mathias says: Notice the differences and similarities between attack banding and defense banding. An attacking band can include no more than one creature without banding ability, and the controller of the band determines how damage is distributed among members of the band. There isn't really any such thing as a "defending band"; multiple creatures can always block a single attacker, whether any of them have banding or not. The banding rules only apply if there's at least one banding creature among the blocking creatures when it's time to distribute damage; then, as in attack banding, the controller of the banding creature gets to determine how damage is distributed among the blockers. In both cases, the controller of the banding creatures can put all the damage on one creature if he or she wishes. This is particularly effective if you have a creature with the regeneration ability in the band; you can assign all the damage to that creature, regenerate, and do the same thing again the following turn. But watch out for trample damage; if you assign all the trample damage to one creature in the band, then anything beyond what it takes to kill that creature spills over onto you.*

## Protection

A creature with protection from a particular color of magic gains the following abilities: Any damage dealt to the creature by a source of that color is reduced to 0, and the creature cannot be blocked by creatures of that color. The creature cannot be the target of a spell or effect of that color, though it can be affected by spells or effects of that color that do not target it specifically (see **Targets** for more information). Any enchantments of that color already on the creature are dispelled, and no further enchantments of that color may be cast on that creature. In all other cases, the protected creature interacts normally with cards of that color.

*Selene says: Suppose I have a Black Knight, which has protection from white, and I'm being attacked by a band of Benalish Heroes, which are white creatures. I can block the Heroes with the Black Knight, and it won't take any damage from them. If it's my turn, I can attack with the Black Knight and the Heroes can't block it. The Black Knight cannot be the target of any white spells or effects, no matter which player casts them; its protection from white covers not only spells that would hurt it, like Swords to Plowshares, but also spells that would help it, like Holy Strength and Death Ward. However, it is affected by white spells that neither do damage nor specifically target it; one example of this would be Wrath of God, which destroys all creatures in play. I can also use a white Healing Salve spell to prevent damage to my Black Knight; in this case, the spell targets the damage, not the creature it's damaging. Likewise, the damage the Black Knight does can be stopped by white cards like Healing Salve and Circle of Protection: Black, since those cards also target the damage the Black Knight is doing rather than the Black Knight itself. Finally, white enchantments on other nonwhite creatures do affect the Black Knight if it interacts with those creatures; for example, a red creature with the white Holy Strength enchantment would still receive the enchantment's bonus to its power and toughness when blocking or being blocked by the Black Knight.*

*Mathias says: If my attacking Benalish Heroes are banded together with a nonwhite creature, say a Hill Giant, a defending Black Knight still takes no damage from the Heroes, but does take damage from the Giant. I can assign the damage from the Knight to a Hero, the Giant, or some to each. Now let's turn this around and have the Black Knight attacking. The Giant can block the Knight, but the Heroes cannot; they can't form a "defensive band" with the Giant, since banding ability has absolutely no effect on defense unless at least one creature with banding legally blocks. For our final example, let's give the Knight's controller a Hero too. If the Knight and the Hero band together for an attack— which is perfectly legal—then the Knight can be blocked by the defending Heroes, since it's banded with a creature that the Heroes can block. The Knight's controller will probably choose to assign all of the blockers' damage to the Knight, since it's immune to the white Heroes' damage.*

# Visiting the Graveyard

## Destroyed, Buried, and Removed from Game

If a spell or effect says it *destroys* or *kills* another card, the target card is sent to the graveyard, though it may be regenerated by an appropriate spell or effect before it gets there. If a spell or effect says it *buries* another card, the target card is put in the graveyard and cannot be regenerated.

*Mathias says: A spell that kills, destroys, or buries a creature directly is not quite the same as one that does so by doing damage. Spells that prevent damage, like Healing Salve, won't help against effects that destroy a creature directly. If a creature has protection from red, it can't be damaged by red spells whether they're targeted or not, but a red spell that destroys creatures directly without damaging them will still affect it as long as the spell doesn't target the creature specifically.*

Some spells and effects remove other cards from the game entirely. Such cards do not go into the graveyard, but into a separate pile. They are returned to their owners only at the end of the duel. Such cards are *not* considered either dead or buried unless the card that caused the removal says otherwise.

*Selene says: Any enchantments on the creature that is removed from the game go back into their owners' graveyards when the creature is removed from the game, unless the card that caused the removal says otherwise.*

## Saving Creatures from the Grave

Whenever a creature is assigned damage, you have the opportunity to use effects that prevent or redirect some or all of the damage. Such effects target the damage, not the source or recipient of the damage. If after this the creature has still taken lethal damage, you can use effects to regenerate it. Remember that damage is cumulative, and further damage this turn may send the creature to the graveyard again. During this period, only damage prevention effects, damage redirection effects, regeneration effects, and interrupts may be used.

*Mathias says: For example, the spell Healing Salve will prevent up to 3 points of damage to a creature. You can use Healing Salve on a creature even if it has protection from white, since the spell targets the damage, not the creature. If you don't have a Healing Salve handy, you could cast Death Ward, which regenerates the creature. That'll bring it back to full power and toughness, including any bonuses from fast effects used earlier in the turn. All enchantments on the creature stay on it, and its little trip to the graveyard gates does not count as a death for the purposes of spells or effects that go off when a creature dies. But if the creature ends up with 0 toughness even after it has been regenerated, it dies again immediately.*

## The Graveyard

When a card reaches the graveyard, any enchantments on it are removed, as are any counters. Cards in the graveyard have no "memory" of previous events, such as how many times they were used or what put them in the graveyard.

*Selene says: Enchantments that are removed always go to their owners' graveyards. If you later remove a card from the graveyard with a spell or effect that brings it to your hand, treat it exactly as if you just drew it from your library. If the spell or effect puts it back into play instead of into your hand, the card comes out as if it*

*had just been cast; if it has an X in the casting cost, it comes out with X equal to 0. Some cards will thus end up with 0 toughness, in which case they die instantly and go right back to the graveyard.*

## The Color of Spells and Effects

The color of the mana in the casting cost of a card determines the color of the spell; if the card is a permanent, it also determines the color of any effects generated by the card. If a spell does not require any particular color of mana to be cast, it and its effects are considered colorless. You can also use the borders of the cards to tell the color of a spell at a glance.

*Mathias says: Some spells can change the color of a card. Such spells change only the color of the card itself, not the color of any mana it or any of its abilities may require. For example, the Frozen Shade is a black card that uses black mana to power a special ability. If a spell turns the Shade green, it still requires black mana to power its special ability, but the Shade itself is no longer black. Among other things, that means it isn't affected by Bad Moon (which gives black creatures +1/+1) and its damage cannot be prevented by a Circle of Protection: Black.*

Remember that although land cards are sources of colored mana, they themselves are colorless. Also, damage taken from excess mana is damage from a colorless source, no matter what color mana is left over or what color of card the extra mana came from.

*Selene says: Yes, you can cast a color-changing spell on a land.
Doing so has no effect on the mana produced by the land, but
it might make the land itself vulnerable to different spells.*

## Sources of Damage

The *source* of a given amount of damage is the card that
dealt that damage, whether or not another card enabled it to
do so. For example, Creature Bond does damage to the controller of a creature if that creature is destroyed. The source
of this damage would be the Creature Bond card, not the
creature or the card that destroyed the creature.

Likewise, if a spell or effect modifies a creature's power, the
color of any damage done by the creature remains the color
of the creature, not the color of the modifying card. Damage
done by a green creature with a red enchantment that
increases its power is considered damage from a green source.

*Mathias says: A few examples: Damage from a Creature
Bond is blue damage, no matter what color the Bonded
creature or the effect that killed it was. Damage from a red
creature with Howl from Beyond cast on it is red, not
black, and thus will damage creatures with protection from
black. Damage from a white creature with Firebreathing
cast on it is white, not red; it can be stopped by Circle of
Protection: White but not by Circle of Protection: Red.*

## Timing

The timing of spells is occasionally rather tricky. You and
your opponent might both want to do something at the

same time, or counteract a counteraction, or something equally complicated. When you read the timing rules to follow, please keep in mind that you should never be in a race to see who can announce a spell first. If your opponent is checking with you after every step, or at least moving slowly enough that you can jump in if you want to, you shouldn't ever have to pounce to get a spell cast.

*Selene says: Remember, if there's any possibility you might want to use a fast effect, you can say, "Wait," and your opponent has to stop and give you time to think about it. Once you've made up your mind, either announce your action or just say, "Go on." When casting your own spells, always go slowly enough that your opponent has a chance to ask you to wait.*

If both players want to announce spells, the player whose turn it is announces spells first. Except for fast effects, spells occur one after the other, so one spell gets to finish casting before another starts.

*Mathias says: This means you can't cast a summon spell and simultaneously cast an enchantment to strengthen or protect the creature. Once the summon is cast, your opponent can use a fast effect to kill the creature before you can enchant it.*

## Resolving Existing Effects

Before resolving the effects of spells or fast effects, you must apply any existing effects that might affect the situation. Existing effects include the continuous effects of permanents and the effects of spells and fast effects that have already been resolved. Apply all existing effects in the order that they occured, then apply current spells and fast effects (see the following rules). Do not determine if a creature has died until all effects have been applied.

## Interrupts and Timing

Interrupts, which are considered fast effects, are resolved immediately after casting unless they are interrupted themselves. Don't actually cut in when someone is announcing an interrupt; wait until your opponent finishes, then announce an interrupt of your own. Remember, players are always obliged to give their opponents a chance to cast spells in response to their actions. If a spell is the target of more than one interrupt, then the player who cast that spell resolves his or her interrupts of that spell first, no matter in what order the interrupts were cast. If Interrupt A is cast and then Interrupt B targets A, Interrupt B takes effect first.

 *Selene says: For example, I cast a Fireball. I interrupt my Fireball with a Fork, a spell that creates an exact copy of any sorcery or instant spell, while Mathias interrupts the Fireball with a Blue Elemental Blast, which would counter the Fireball spell. It doesn't matter which of us gets an interrupt off first; the Fork will happen first, since I cast it and I'm the one who cast the original spell. In the end, the Fireball spell generated by my Fork will go off, but my original Fireball will be countered by Mathias's Blue Elemental Blast.*

## Other Fast Effects and Timing

Other fast effects include instant spells, creature special abilities, and effects generated by permanents in play.

After your opponent announces a spell or fast effect, you may respond with one or more fast effects. Your opponent may then respond by announcing fast effects in return, and then you may respond, until nobody wants to cast any more. Once all effects have been announced, then each one takes effect, starting with the *last* effect announced. Fast effects other than interrupts are resolved last to first. However, you don't apply damage or determine whether a creature is dead or not until all fast effects in the chain have been resolved.

*Mathias says: Let's say that Selene casts another Fireball, this time aimed at my Craw Wurm (6/4). Fireball is a sorcery, so she has to decide at the time she casts it how much mana she will spend on it; she can't increase it later. She pumps in enough mana to make the spell do 4 points of damage, enough to kill the Wurm unless I do something. I respond by casting an instant called Giant Growth on the Wurm, giving it +3/+3 to save it from the Fireball. Selene taps another mountain and casts an instant called Lightning Bolt, doing 3 more points of damage to the Wurm. Neither of us announces any more fast effects for this exchange, so now all of the fast effects are resolved in reverse order. The Wurm takes 3 points of damage from the Lightning Bolt, gains +3/+3 from the Giant Growth, and then takes 4 points of damage from the Fireball. It ends up with 7 toughness and 7 damage, so it heads toward the graveyard. At this point, I could cast a Death Ward on the Wurm, regenerating it; it would then come back as a tapped 9/7 creature. If I had had an Unsummon spell, also an instant, I could have cast it in response to the Lightning Bolt; the Wurm would then have gone back to my hand before any damage was done to it.*

## Resolving Fast Effects

Usually, this process is merely a matter of following the instructions on the card. It is very important to remember that unless a fast effect is *countered* by an interrupt, it will take effect no matter what else happens (see **Countering Effects** for more information on countering). Even if the source of a fast effect is destroyed during the resolution of these effects, the fast effect itself will succeed. For example, if you use a Rod of Ruin to do a point of damage to your opponent and your opponent responds by casting the instant Shatter on the Rod, then you resolve these fast effects last to first—the Shatter is resolved, sending the Rod to the graveyard, and then the Rod's effect occurs, doing a point of damage.

*Selene says: Prodigal Sorcerers work the same way. If I have a Prodigal Sorcerer on the table and Mathias casts Terror on it, I can still tap the Sorcerer to do 1 last point of damage as it goes to the graveyard.*

*Mathias says: Remember way back near the beginning, when the rules said that tapping land counts as an interrupt? Now I can explain why that's important. Suppose Selene casts a Stone Rain to destroy one of my lands. I can tap my lands, including the one she's trying to destroy, and use the mana to power a Counterspell to save the land. If tapping land was a fast effect instead of an interrupt, this wouldn't work.*

*Selene says: That reminds me of another loose end I promised to explain. If you cast Twiddle on one of my lands, thinking that you can tap it and thereby prevent me from getting mana from it, I can simply interrupt your Twiddle to tap the land myself and draw the mana*

*into my mana pool. The Twiddle then has no effect,*
*since it's essentially tapping a card that's already tapped.*

## Countering Effects

Some interrupts will *counter* other spells or effects. If a
spell or fast effect is countered, the cost of the effect is
not refunded, but the spell or effect fails to occur.
Countered spells go to the graveyard. Countering an
effect with an interrupt is the only way to prevent that
effect from happening.

*Mathias says: If I spend* 🌑 *+* 8 *to Disintegrate*
*one of Selene's creatures and she casts Blue Elemental*
*Blast to counter it, the Disintegrate card goes to my*
*graveyard without damaging her creature, but my*
*mana is still spent.*

## Failed Spells and Missing Targets

You cannot cast a targeted spell or use a targeted fast effect
unless there is a valid target for it at the time it is
announced. Sometimes interfering with a card's target is as
good as countering it. Some spells don't need targets (see
**Targets** for more information).

Sometimes an interrupt, instant, or other fast effect
causes the only legal target of an effect or spell to disappear or become illegal after the effect or spell is
announced but before it takes place. In this case, the mana

is spent and the spell is cast for no effect. If a spell has multiple legal targets when declared, and some of the targets disappear before it takes effect, its effect on the remaining targets is unchanged. All of its legal targets must disappear for it to fail.

*Selene says: This does not mean that you can change the target or targets of a spell after it is cast. So, let's say Mathias has two Merfolk in play and an Unsummon card in his hand. If I cast a Lightning Bolt at one of the Merfolk, Mathias can cast Unsummon on the Merfolk to rescue it. The Lightning Bolt just goes away; I cannot change it to aim at the other Merfolk. Now suppose instead that I cast Fireball, spending enough mana to do 1 point of damage to each of the two Merfolk and 1 point to Mathias. Again Mathias casts Unsummon on one of the Merfolk, returning it to his hand. The other Merfolk and Mathias still take 1 point of damage apiece. I cannot recalculate the spell and do 2 points of damage to each of them, and I cannot aim the part of the damage that targeted the missing Merfolk at a different creature.*

## Responding to Spells

If the current player fails to give his opponent a chance to act before moving to the next phase or casting the next spell, the opponent may require him to take back his most recent action, moving the game backwards to the appropriate phase. But if the opponent has allowed the current player to take multiple actions, this is considered tacit agreement that she did not wish to take any further actions in the previous phase.

*Mathias says: This is why it's so important to say "Wait!" if there's any chance you might want to respond to something your opponent has done. If you let your opponent go on while you think about it, your opportunity to respond will probably be gone by the time you've made up your mind.*

 *Selene says: All the rest of this is examples, so Mathias and I will sign off now. Hope our comments were helpful!*

# Example of Creature Combat

## Attack and Fast Effects

Carol is attacking, Miguel defending. Carol announces an attack and taps the following creatures: a Hill Giant (3/3) enchanted with Flight, a Dryad (1/1, forestwalk), a War Mammoth (3/3, trample), and a Sea Serpent (5/5, can't attack unless opponent has islands in play). Miguel has two Benalish Heroes (1/1, bands), a Unicorn (2/2), a Prodigal Sorcerer (1/1 with special damage ability), and an Ogre (2/2) with the Firebreathing enchantment. Miguel has both forests and islands in play on his side.

Miguel's islands allow Carol's Sea Serpent to attack. His forest allows Carol's Dryad to forestwalk, so it can't be blocked by any of his creatures. Since the Giant is flying and none of Miguel's creatures can fly, his creatures can't block the Giant either. Now that Carol has announced her attackers, Miguel casts Jump, an instant that gives a creature flying ability, on one of his Heroes. Carol declines to cast any fast effects.

## Defense and Fast Effects

Now Miguel declares defense. He assigns the Jumping Hero to block the Giant, the Unicorn and the Sorcerer to block the Mammoth, and the other Hero and the Ogre to block the Serpent. At this point, Carol can see some probable outcomes. The first Hero will do 1 point of damage to the Giant, which can take 3. The Giant will kill the Hero in return, doing 3 points of damage to a creature that can only take 1. The two creatures blocking the Mammoth are going to do enough combined damage to kill the Mammoth, but the Mammoth could kill both blockers in return. Carol decides to change this and casts Giant Growth on her Mammoth, giving it +3/+3.

Miguel now expects that when damage time comes around, the Mammoth will do 3 points of damage to kill the two blockers; because the Mammoth has the trample ability, the other 3 points will strike him. Furthermore, the Mammoth now has an increased toughness, so the two blockers will no longer be able to kill it. The Sorcerer's special ability is to do 1 point of damage to any target, so Miguel decides to use this ability one last time before the Sorcerer bites the dust. Miguel has the Sorcerer do 1 point of damage to the Dryad, killing it and leaving the Sorcerer tapped.

Miguel also looks at Carol's Serpent and sees that, right now, his blocking creatures will only do 3 points of damage while the Serpent has a toughness of 5. He taps two mountains to provide 🔴 🔴 for the Firebreathing enchantment on the Ogre. The Ogre is now effectively a 4/2 creature, so combined with the Hero it can kill the Serpent.

Finally, there's Carol's Giant. Miguel doesn't have a spell to save the Jumping Hero, but he does have Howl from Beyond, an instant that increases a creature's power by an amount that depends on how much mana the player spends. He plays the card on his Hero and taps enough land to give the Hero a +5 bonus. Adding +2 would be enough to kill the Giant, but Miguel wants to make sure that a Healing Salve, which prevents 3 points of damage, would be insufficient to save the Giant. Unlike the enchantment Firebreathing, for which the activation cost can be paid multiple times, the power of Howl from Beyond is set when it is cast and cannot be changed.

## Damage and Saving Dying Creatures

Both players agree they're done with fast effects, so now they assign damage. As expected, the Giant does 3 points of damage to the Hero blocking it, which has a toughness of 1. The Hero is quite dead. With its Howl from Beyond, it did 6 points of damage in return, which finishes off the Giant.

The Mammoth deals 6 points of trample damage to its blockers. Carol assigns all 6 to the Sorcerer. One point is sufficient to kill it, so the other 5 are subtracted from Miguel's life point total. The Unicorns are unharmed. The Unicorns do 2 points of damage to the Mammoth in return, but the Sorcerer does no damage in return since it is now tapped.

The Serpent does 5 points of damage to the Ogre and Hero blocking it. Because the Hero has banding, Miguel gets to decide where that damage goes, not Carol. He chooses to have all 5 points of damage go to the Hero, killing it but leaving the Ogre unharmed. The Hero and Ogre do 5 points of damage in return, killing the Serpent.

Now it's time for damage redirection, damage prevention, and regeneration. Carol casts Death Ward on her Serpent, regenerating it. All other creatures who took lethal damage are put in their owners' graveyards.

# Example of Spell Combat

Chris has Grizzly Bears, a 2/2 creature, in play. Leyla casts Terror on the Bears, which would bury them. In response Chris casts Unsummon on the Bears, which would bring them back to his hand. Neither player decides to use any more fast effects. The spells are now resolved in reverse order. First the Unsummon happens, so the Bears go back to Chris's hand. Now Terror goes off; its target is now gone, so the spell fails and is discarded. If Chris had decided to Unsummon the Bears and in response Leyla had cast Terror, or if a second Terror had been cast after the Unsummon, the Bears would have been buried.

# Applying the Rules

## Cards that Break the Rules

Some cards may grant abilities that conflict with the rules. These cards always take precedence.

## Old Rules

Earlier versions of *Magic: The Gathering* had slightly different sets of rules. There have been many subtle changes between previous sets and this revised set. We strongly encourage anybody who has played using any other set of rules to read this new set carefully and at least twice, so you aren't surprised when somebody else plays differently. Since the card wordings and the rules are closely linked, mixing cards between versions could also cause peculiar side effects, which you should be prepared to discuss with your opponent ahead of time.

# DIFFERENCES BETWEEN FIRST EDITION AND REVISED EDITION MAGIC: THE GATHERING RULES

*Beth Moursund*

Most of the changes in the Revised Edition of *Magic: The Gathering* are cosmetic, clarifying the old rules but not changing the meaning. A few, however, are actual rule changes; these were done in cases where the original rules turned out to be paradoxical, contradictory, or confusing (even to the designers). Players who learned the game under the First Edition rules need to be aware of these changes.

## ⚙ SYMBOL and ARTIFACTS

Revised Edition cards use a new symbol, ⚙ , when tapping a card is included in the cost of an effect. For example, instead of "Tap to do 1 damage to any target," a card would say " ⚙ : do 1 damage to any target." This eliminates the distinction between "mono" and "poly" artifacts—a First Edition "mono artifact" becomes an artifact with ⚙ as part of its activation cost, while a First Edition "poly artifact" becomes an artifact with no ⚙ in the cost, and a First Edition "continuous artifact" becomes an artifact with no activation cost.

## DEFINITIONS

### "BURIED"

The Revised Edition uses the term "bury" to mean "send

something to the Graveyard with no regeneration allowed."

## "TARGET"

This is another term that the First Edition used but didn't actually define. If the user of a spell or effect chooses which card(s) are affected by it, then that effect *targets* those cards, and it won't affect a Protected creature. If the user doesn't get to choose—for example, a spell that affects "all flying creatures" or "all blue creatures"—then the effect is not targeted, and Protection won't stop it. (If the non-targeted effect does damage, Protection can still reduce the damage to zero.)

## "DEFENDING CREATURES"

In the First Edition, the term "defending creature" was not precisely defined, but it was used in a way that implied "any creature on the defending side during an attack, whether blocking or not." Under the Revised rules, "defending creature" is synonymous with "blocking creature." This changes the valid targets for a few spells.

# PROTECTION

The First Edition rules for the creature ability Protection from *Color* were overly broad and somewhat ambiguous, which produced a number of problems. Forget everything you knew about Protection. The new definition of the creature ability Protection from *Color* is:

- Any damage dealt to the creature by a *Color* source is reduced to 0. This includes Trample damage.

- The creature cannot be blocked by *Color* creatures.
- The creature cannot be the target of a *Color* spell or effect. This includes creature special effects, like the Nettling Imp. It also means that *Color* Enchantment Creature cannot be cast on that creature.
- Any *Color* enchantments already on the creature are dispelled.
- The creature can be affected by *Color* spells or effects that do not do damage or target it, such as Wrath of God.
- Damage done by this creature can be prevented by *Color* spells and effects, since they target the damage, not the creature.

# THE ATTACK SEQUENCE

The Revised Edition cleans up the attack sequence a bit, setting restrictions on when you may and may not use fast effects. The attack sequence is now broken down as follows:

1. Announce attack; last chance for either player to use pre-attack fast effects.
2. Declare and tap attacking creatures.
3. Either player may use fast effects.
4. Declare blocking.
5. Either player may use fast effects. Note that if a blocking creature is removed or a blocked attacking creature rendered unblockable during this segment, the attacking creature is still blocked.
6. Assign damage.
7. Either player may use damage-prevention, damage-redirection, and/or regeneration fast effects. The only other fast effects that may be used at this time are Interrupts and effects feeding off the other spells cast at this time.

8. Creatures that have lethal damage go to the Graveyard.

9. Any effects triggered by the deaths (Vampires gaining counters, Creature Bond damage, Soul Net may be used, and so on) take place. Only fast effects triggered by the deaths may be used.

Note that steps 2, 4, 6, and 8 are considered instantaneous, and you may not use any fast effects during them.

Steps 6–9 happen twice if the combat includes any creatures with the First Strike ability. Steps 6–9 also happen any time that any spell or fast effect causes damage.

## TIMING

Instants no longer take place simultaneously. Instead, after one player announces (and pays for) a spell or fast effect, the other player can respond by announcing fast effects of their own, then the first player again, then the second, and so on, until neither player has any more fast effects they wish to use at that time. Once they've all been announced, they then take effect in reverse order (starting with the last effect announced). Creatures damaged by these fast effects do not go to the Graveyard immediately; instead, after all the fast effects have been resolved, there is a damage-resolution step exactly like that at the end of an Attack, where damage prevention/redirection and regeneration may be used, after which any creature that still has lethal damage goes to the Graveyard.

If one of the effects in the sequence moves a creature off the playing area (either to the Graveyard, back to a player's hand, or out of the game entirely) or in any other way makes it an illegal target for an effect, later effects (i.e., cast earlier) will not move it from that location or affect it. For example, if I cast Terror on a creature and you respond with Unsummon, the Unsummon moves the creature to your hand and so Terror can't move it to the Graveyard. If you cast Unsummon first and I respond with Terror, the Terror moves the creature to the Graveyard and the Unsummon can't move it to your hand. Note that such removal does *not* prevent other effects from happening; for example, if I tap a Prodigal Sorcerer to do a point of damage to you, and you cast Terror on him, the Sorcerer goes to the Graveyard and then you take a point of damage.

If a creature is no longer in play when the damage-resolution comes around, then the damage is ignored.

Under these rules, fast effects no longer cause "paradox" situations, so the "paradox" rule has been removed.

## USE OF FAST EFFECTS

In the First Edition, the rules said that fast effects could be used "at any time." This turned out to cause a number of problems and paradoxes, so the Revised rules have removed that definition, and instead specify when fast effects may be used. In addition to the times specified above under **The Attack Sequence**, fast effects may be used during the Upkeep phase and the Main phase, including at the end of the Main Phase in response to an opponent announcing "done." They may not be used during the Untap phase.

Any damage done during the Untap phase may be prevented or redirected at the beginning of the Upkeep phase. Cards that required payment of mana to untap during the Untap phase now untap during the Upkeep phase instead.

# SACRIFICE

Under the Revised rules, a sacrifice is a cost that cannot be prevented, and the card goes to the Graveyard immediately, at the speed of an Interrupt. If a fast effect involves sacrificing a creature, put the creature in the Graveyard as soon as the fast effect is announced, rather than waiting until all other fast effects are announced. (Any benefit or result from the sacrifice still waits until its proper place in the effect-resolution sequence.) Even if the spell or effect is countered in some way, the card being sacrificed still gets buried, just as the mana spent on a countered spell is still spent.

# ENCHANTMENTS THAT BECOME INVALID

Under First Edition rules, an Enchantment stayed around until dispelled, even if the thing it was enchanting changed to something no longer valid for that enchantment. Under the Revised rules, the Enchantment is placed in the Graveyard when this happens. For example, an artifact has an Animate Artifact cast on it, making it a creature artifact. Now you can cast Enchant Creature spells on it. If the Animate is removed, all of the Enchant Creatures must be removed as well.

# WINNING THE GAME

In the Revised Edition, you lose only if your life points are below 1 at the end of a phase or at the start or end of an attack. You can go below zero and then cast a spell to save yourself—even a Sorcery or Enchantment, if it's your own main phase and not during an attack. As in the First Edition, you also lose at any time you're required to draw a card and have none left in your Library.

# CARD ERRATA

Most of the First Edition cards can be played "as is" under the Revised rules. Some Revised cards have minor changes in what they do when compared to First Edition; when playing with mixed sets, play each card by the wording on the card itself. However, just because one version of a card says something explicitly and another version doesn't, this does not mean that they function differently. Some of the card texts contain reminders of things that are already part of the rules. The presence or lack of such text on one card versus another should not be interpreted as meaning that the rule does not apply.

A few cards do need their wording changed, as follows:

These cards say "discard" and should say "destroy": Bottle of Suleiman, Balance, Black Lotus, Chaos Orb, City in a Bottle, Conversion, Cyclone, Disenchant, Drop of Honey, Jihad, Pestilence, Tranquility, Unsummon.

Many of the earlier cards do not use the word "target." A spell or effect is targeted if the user can have any choice in what it affects. For example, Simulacrum and Volcanic Eruption are targeted; Wrath of God and the power of the Thicket Basilisk are not. Animate Dead and Earthbind are both "Enchant Creature." (Earthbind can be cast upon a non-flying creature, but only does damage if cast upon a flying creature.)

All cards that refer to "loss of life" should be read as "damage to player" except: Channel, Lich, Personal Incarnation, and Shahrazad. Damage from those four cards may not be prevented or redirected. All other damage to a player may be.

Any cards that do something "at start of turn" do it during the Upkeep phase. Any cards that function "every upkeep" affect each player during their own Upkeep phase only. Paralyzed creatures untap during the Upkeep phase. Power Surge counts lands before untapping, but does damage during Upkeep.

Iron Star, Throne of Bone, Ivory Cup, Wooden Sphere, Urza's Chalice, and Crystal Rod may be used during the damage-prevention step of an attack.

Add a 🍥 to the cost for all Mono Artifacts.

# IV

## Developing Your Deck

### •Deck Tuning

Jim Lin, one of the original playtesters, discusses the common mistakes of beginning deck builders and offers some pointers on nudging your deck towards strategic perfection.

### •Now That You Have Your Killer Deck...

As Richard Garfield explains, the play environment that you adopt can have a major impact on the effectiveness of your deck and your enjoyment of the game.

# Deck Tuning

*Jim Lin*

Some of you out there may be a little frustrated. After all, you know that you're a much better **Magic** player than your next door neighbor, but he went out and bought five display boxes of booster packs, and now it doesn't seem like you have any chance to win anymore. Well, both you and your neighbor may be in for a little surprise. Probably the most fascinating aspect of **Magic** is figuring out neat combinations of cards, and then collecting the right cards, not just the most cards. If you do this properly, and your next door neighbor doesn't, you may find that his five boxes of boosters are just a source of free cards for you. Yes, it's always better to own more cards, but a little skill and forethought will go a long way toward making the number of cards you own less important.

Since figuring out rare combinations is one of the enjoyable and challenging aspects of Magic, we don't intend to spoil the fun. Instead of listing card combinations, this chapter presents some basic principles for building decks. If you think about how these rules apply to the way you have been playing and the cards you have been playing with, and make the proper adjustments, your win rate should increase dramatically.

## How Many Cards Should I Play With, And How Many Kinds?

One of the most common mistakes is to play with all of your Magic cards. Beyond the obvious difficulty of shuffling hundreds of cards, the fact is that some cards are much more useful or powerful than others. Since you probably have limited resources, it is easier to get a small number of those cards than it is to get a lot of them, which means that unless you are willing to spend an exorbitant amount of money buying Magic cards to increase the percentage of these coveted cards in your deck, it's difficult to construct a killer deck of two hundred cards, or even sixty cards. When in doubt, try to stay as close to the forty-card minimum limit as possible. There is a very good reason that there is a minimum card limit but no maximum card limit. You may find that as you are cutting the size of your deck down, you will stop using cards that seemed pretty powerful to you. If you do this right, though, you won't miss them, no matter how much it seems like you will.

Playing with fewer cards also allows you more control over the games you are playing. Adding more cards to your deck is like adding a randomizer to it. If you are serious about winning a lot, you shouldn't be willing to "roll the dice" each game. You want to know—not hope—that you are going to get a certain card when you need it. This also means that you should hesitate before putting only one of any card in your deck, because you are adding a random factor back in again. (How likely is it that you will draw that card? When you draw that card, how often will it help you win the game and how often will it just sit in your hand? If you really need that card, how much are you going to be hurt if you lose that card as ante?) It's much safer to play with many cards of a few types, because losing any one of them won't hurt your deck all that much. Naturally, there are some cards that are so powerful, it is worth it to break this rule. Also, many cards are similar enough that while you may only put one of each in, you can really count that as two or three of the same type of card.

## How Many Colors Should I Use?

As you might have guessed, playing with fewer colors has some big advantages. You are much more likely to have enough land to play your spells when you are playing with fewer colors. Naturally, playing with only one color is pretty risky since there are so many cards, such as Circles of Protection, that punish people who specialize too much. Also, all of the colors are deficient in one area or another. Playing one color will probably leave you wide open to the right kind of opponent.

In general, most nasty decks use two colors. If you work at it, you might be able to make three colors or one color work right. Four or five colors is almost out of the question. Choosing the right colors to play with is mostly a function of personal style. Some people enjoy playing destructive cards and gravitate towards red magic. Others like having lots of creatures and tend towards green. Experiment with the colors a little bit and see which colors fit your temperament.

## How Much Land Do I Need?

Most beginners make the mistake of not playing with enough land in their decks. The simplest way to judge this is as follows: if you find that you usually can't play more than half of the cards in your hand because you don't have enough mana, then you are playing with too few land cards, or too many expensive cards, or both. Another good way of gauging the amount of land you are playing with is to look at the number of cards in your hand when you reach turn three or four. If you have the proper mix of land, and both cheap and expensive cards, then your hand should be well on its way to zero cards by now. You will probably have some cards in hand since you are saving them for a better situation, but you should laugh at cards like Black Vise or Library of Leng. If you are ever in danger of taking a significant amount of damage from a Black Vise or needing the power of the Library of Leng, then you should play with more land and less expensive cards.

Your own experience and how much difficulty you have in playing cards should be the final word in determining how much land to play with. Generally, however, playing with a deck that is anything less than one-third land is probably suicidal except for very special cases (such as a deck in which every spell costs one mana). When laying out the cards you are planning to play with, lay out lands to match them. Spells that provide mana can be thought of as supporting themselves, as long as you have a decent number of other cards in that color. Cards that cost only one mana to be put into play can probably be supported at slightly better than two cards for every one land, perhaps something like five cards for every two lands. Any card that requires more than one of a specific color of mana, or requires that colored mana be spent on a regular basis to use it, should probably be supported with one whole land. The rest of the cards can probably be supported at a rate of two cards for one land. You can overdo it—after all, it's impossible to kill your opponent if you are doing nothing but laying down a land every turn—but usually the rule is: when in doubt, throw in more land. If worse comes to worse, throwing in more land will just make it more likely that you will ante land. Land is cheap; take advantage of that fact.

# Are Little, Cheap Cards or Big, Expensive Cards Better?

This is a much tougher question to answer. At the heart of this question lie two basic facts of the game. First and foremost, **Magic** is a race to see who can kill their opponent first. Speed can definitely be deadly. If you kill your opponent every game by turn six, then your opponent's Shivan Dragon won't help him much, since he usually won't be able to summon the Dragon until turn six. Even if you don't kill them on turn six, you may be able to drive him to such a low life level that even his Dragon won't save him by the time it comes into play.

Since speed kills, you will find that any card that allows you to gain mana early in the game will be very valuable. These cards allow you to get around one of the basic limitations of the game: you can only play one land per turn. This is also another reason why you tend not to play with single copies of a card: you don't intend the game to last very long. After all, the winner is the first person to kill their opponent, not the person who kills his opponent most completely or most impressively. If you don't expect to see a card until after turn ten or turn fifteen, then you might as well not see it— you or your opponent should be dead by the time you draw it. This is also why the threat of running out of cards rarely plays any part in the game. Unless you or your opponent has a deck designed specifically only to stop the other player, and not kill the other player (and it is possible to build those), one of you just won't last that long.

Does this mean you shouldn't be playing with those big creatures? No. The other basic limitation on a game of **Magic** is the number of cards you see. Unless you arrange a way to draw more cards, by the end of the first turn you can't play more than eight cards. That's not much of a limitation, but saying that by the end of turn seven you won't be able to play more than fourteen cards is very limiting. (Naturally, the ability to draw more cards allows you to get around this restriction, and can be extremely valuable.) This constraint on the number of cards you can play means that you want the cards you get into play to remain in play for a while. If you rely on too many inexpensive cards that are played and then discarded, you may jump out to an early lead, but when your opponent's bigger, meaner cards that are reusable come into play, the game can rapidly swing back in the other direction.

Any card that allows you to use it over and over is very valuable. Many beginning players, for example, discount the utility of creatures. After all, when there are things like Fireball and Disintegrate floating around out there, why bother with a piddly three or four points of damage? The simple answer is that pound for pound, card for card, creatures are the most efficient way of doing damage to your

opponent. Theoretically, a creature can deal a huge amount of damage to your opponent if given enough time. As a general guideline, if you have any spell or effect that allows you to do damage to any target, you should always hesitate before choosing your opponent as that target. Obviously, if you are about to kill your opponent, go right ahead—that is the object of the game, after all. In many cases, however, it is much more efficient to use your direct damage card to kill some of opponent's creatures to allow your creatures to deal even more damage to your opponent.

On a similar note, be wary of playing in a way that allows opponent to destroy many of your cards with a single blow. That will leave you without much firepower. For example, you may be able to pile up enough enchantments on your creature so that he is now 10/10 with +1/0 for every red mana, and so on, but when your opponent plays Terror and kills that creature, you are going to be left with no cards in your hand and no cards in play, while your opponent has plenty of cards left to play and kill you with. Of course, if they don't kill the creature somehow, they aren't going to live very long, are they? You need to balance the risk of losing a lot of cards at once with the gains of being able to kill opponent more quickly. On the flip side, any card that allows you to destroy many of opponent's cards with just that one card is a great card, but you shouldn't wait too long to use it, or else you just might be dead by the time you get around to wreaking havoc.

The basic limitation on the number of cards you get to play in a game also means that when you look at a card, you shouldn't just ask yourself if the ability that card gives you is nice to have, you should compare it with another ability you could have given yourself. Yes, it is nice to be able to look at your opponent's hand and see what is coming and whether they can stop you. However, once you think of all of the other things you could have done instead of looking at your opponent's hand, you may not be all that interested in looking at your opponent's hand anymore. Don't think "Glasses of Urza allows me to look at my opponent's hand," but rather "Glasses of Urza prevents me from summoning my Dragon Whelp or zapping my opponent's Wraith with a Lightning Bolt because I drew Glasses of Urza instead of those cards." As a general guideline, before putting any card in your deck, ask yourself whether there is any situation in which you would want that card to be in your hand more than any other card you own. If there is not, put that card aside, and start looking for new cards to play with. Naturally, whether you want a card or not will depend heavily on the other cards that are in your deck. Certain cards work exceedingly well together.

## When Can I Start?

Once you've assessed your deck's problems and potential, you can formulate your deck-building strategy. Keep in mind both the limits you will have on developing mana and drawing cards. It may take you a lot of experimenting to come up with a combination of cards that will work well together and allow you to win on a regular basis early in the game. Remember, don't limit your thinking to the card pool you own. One of the most satisfying portions of building a good deck is going out and finding someone who has that crucial card, and trading or winning it from them. If no one you regularly play with has the card, try to find new people to play with. They might just have that card, or others you haven't considered—and it's always fun to encounter the different styles and different ideas about card combinations that new opponents can offer. Don't be afraid of borrowing other people's ideas—or even better, improving upon them.

# Now That You Have Your Killer Deck...

*Richard Garfield*

Anyone who has played **Magic** any length of time has run into it: that irrepressible gleam in the eye that says "my deck is *so good*." The thrill of building and competing these "killer decks" is undeniable. While most beginners start by trying to stuff a bunch of neat toys in their decks, things which worked for or against them in the past, they soon realize that the difficult part is getting these tricks to work consistently. Extremely narrow decks—the decks that rely on one trick or one color—are soon discarded in favor of the real killer decks, the decks that have excellent chances to win against any deck if they go first.

Surrounding this emphasis on power playing is a certain kind of gaming environment. This "wild environment" has no real restrictions on the number or kind of cards you can draw on for deck construction, or on which decks can compete against each other. It is the way the game naturally starts in a play group: glorious free trade and chaos. Among many players, particularly the less competitive ones, this is a great way to play. You can play a deck that you like until boredom sets in and then move on to something else. However, in many groups, the "deck technology" eventually gets too high and people find they can't play as hard as they want to and still have fun games. The games become predictable because the decks have become predictable.

Fortunately, while such decks are a part of the game, they aren't the end of the road. Players tired of pure power playing can choose to reduce their emphasis on constructing decks just to win. This shifts the emphasis away from deck design and toward deck play. After all, the better you are at deck construction, the more the skill in the duel itself is overshadowed, since a really powerful deck tends to be really easy to play. "Can I make a deck better than your deck?" therefore becomes "Can I win with this deck, or something very close to it?"

In a mature wild environment, the deck-design part of the game becomes less of a harsh science and more of an art. People keep decks around not only because the decks win, but because they enjoy playing with them. There is often an array of decks available to each player, and some sort of vague rank associated with each one. Players will pit their decks against one another, tinker with them, and try again. Sure, the heavyweights can trounce the featherweights, but that doesn't mean the featherweights should be banned from play. A featherweight is fun to play and tinker with. And it may take out a lightweight (or even a mediumweight) from time to time.

Some self-enforced rules can be followed in a wild environment to preserve the challenge of deck assembly and dueling. One simple option is to keep one random deck isolated from the rest of your cards. These low-power decks can be freely traded with and pared down, but may not incorporate outside resources. The only way to improve these decks is by trading or dueling with them. If more than one player in your group maintains such low-power decks, the wild environment can be kept interesting, while not reducing the degree of competition.

For players who, in an effort to emphasize the skills of dueling, prefer to keep deck construction more equitable, there is an alternative to the free-for-all of the wild. A more structured environment places restrictions on how players can acquire their initial cards, how trading can be conducted, and usually who can play who and how often. The simplest way to develop a structured environment between two players or within a playgroup is to give each player a random starting deck. This deck could be a factory deck, or one assembled using cards provided by one or more of the players. In this case, decks are built by trading between members of the playgroup rather than by purchasing cards.

A more complex method, but one which better satisfies the player who enjoys the competition of deck construction, is the draft. All the cards are laid on the table and players take turns picking cards for their deck. In a simpler form of the draft, the card set is shuffled and one card is turned up for each player. Each player selects a card; first pick then rotates to another player, and more cards are turned up. To speed up the draft, the cards can be grouped in twos or threes. While some players prefer to keep land out of the draft, others like to make land a limited resource—something that rarely happens in the wild environment.

Another game element which may be restricted is trade. Trading can be a terribly influential factor in the game, and can dominate the competition if it isn't controlled. While some players prefer the free-for-all, others may choose to restrict trading to some time period before or between games, or forbid it altogether. To minimize the danger of someone getting a runaway advantage from good trading, and to prevent short-term loans of important cards, trading is usually only permitted at the start of the competition or at set intervals. You may also decide that all trades must be made public within the playgroup.

Dueling can be structured in a variety of ways. In two-person duels, players usually compete until one participant wins a set number of games. You might also consider the often lengthy but enjoyable challenge of playing for ante until one deck can no longer be reasonably played. Within a larger playgroup, the competition may remain an unstructured set of duels between individuals or teams, or it may build toward a single winner. You may elect to hold a round robin, where each player competes with every other player a certain number of times. Whatever the structure, it is advisable that players duel each other in some regular pattern, so that a single participant doesn't repeatedly encounter a particularly weak or particularly strong deck. Players may be permitted to modify their decks between games or after a set number of duels, or they may have to compete with unaltered decks. If playing for ante, the playgroup may decide that ante must be added to the active decks, which will force players to keep their decks reasonably varied. Alternatively, the ante can be returned to the owners after the contest is finished.

The existence of a structured environment does not preclude the wild environment; indeed, it is enjoyable to play in both, since they emphasize such different aspects of play. The playgroup merely has to keep the cards for each type of play separate. To preserve the integrity of structured play decks, you may choose to mark the cards, or to store the decks in the care of a single player. Serious playgroups have even been known to record the contents of all the decks.

Future versions of **Magic** may keep the wild environment under control by keeping the cards more uniform in strength. These card mixes should help satisfy players who want to preserve deck building as the central challenge without the narrow decks and predictable outcomes that often plague the wild environment. Regardless of the card mix, however, players can improve their game by creating the play environment that best suits their interests.

## Magic: The Gathering Variants

James Ernest provides some possible alternatives you can use to spice up your games. Included are ante variants, mechanics changes, solitaire rules, and rules for three players and five or more players.

## Building a Magic: The Gathering League

Want to start a **Magic** league? Playtester Joel Mick explains how, offering some organizational guidelines and tips on draft structure.

## Team Magic

When two players just aren't enough. Here Jim Lin provides an alternative to the standard two-person duel with a number of variants for team play, including some insights on how the effects of cards change with the addition of teammates.

## Duelists' Convocation Magic Tournament Rules

Steve Bishop, director of the Duelists' Convocation, presents the current rules for officially sanctioned *Magic: The Gathering* tournaments.

# *Magic: The Gathering* **Variants**

*James Ernest*

An innovative game like *Magic: The Gathering* tends to inspire innovation in those who play it. Players and designers alike have come up with a number of interesting variations on the original **Magic** rules, ranging from minor variations on ante, to wild, multiplayer versions of the game.

## **How To Use These Variants**

The following are some of the more popular **Magic** variants. Most of the adaptions for two-player games are straightforward and easily implemented. These are intended to adjust the game towards the varying objectives and skill levels of the players. If you are just learning the game, for example, you might find that the no-ante variants make the duels more enjoyable, but if you are out to improve your deck, you will want to choose a variation that gives you the opportunity to win a card from your opponent. For team and multiplayer **Magic** games, however, there are a huge number of variations, many which involve subtle or complicated rules changes. This chapter presents basic guidelines for some of these variants and suggests areas of the rules to experiment with. Before attempting to play any of them, your play group should explore these areas and discuss the specific rules changes that will apply. In multiplayer games, you will need to determine exactly how each player interacts with the others. For example, can a player affect all other players with his creatures and spells, or just a single opponent? In team games, these concerns are complicated by the degree of communication and cooperation you choose to allow between team members. It will take some experimentation to find the set of rules that suits the interests and skill levels in your play group. Whatever rules you start with, be sure that everyone understands them and is making the same assumptions about game play. The first few times you try out a new variant, it might be a good idea to have someone around who can act as an impartial judge. As always, the most important rule is: have fun. Developing a full-fledged variant can be as enjoyable as playing one; don't hesitate to be innovative!

# The Ante

Many **Magic** players don't like the idea of putting a valuable card at risk each time they play, especially if an opponent antes a land. While some players eliminate the ante altogether, others have developed ways to make it a little less intimidating. When using these ante variants, you should probably consider possible effects of cards that affect the ante, such as Darkpact, and agree in advance how such cards will affect your situation.

## Alter the Ante Selection Process

Instead of making a completely random choice of each others' cards, you might agree on certain limiting conditions. For example:

> **Allow one recut.** If you cut to your opponent's second-favorite card, he can ask you to cut again—but if you now cut to his favorite spell, he'll just have to play well to keep it.

> **Make your most prized cards immune to ante.** For example, you might agree beforehand that if your

only Shatter comes into the ante, you will be allowed to call for another cut instead.

**Recut land cards.** Agree that if either player cuts to a basic land card, they may recut until something interesting comes out instead.

**Alternate pool.** Draw from another pool of cards, instead of your deck. You may want to restrict what can and can't be in this pool.

**Playoff.** Jointly purchase a small number of cards and play a game for each card in the pack. Leave the best ones for last, or keep them all facedown until the end of the game.

**Ante-doubling.** After the ante is drawn, you may choose to replace your contribution with the next two cards in your library. Shuffle the old ante card back into your deck. Some players allow repeated doubling of the ante. If you don't wish to lose the pair, you can swap them for the next four cards, and so on, as long as you still have forty cards to play with. (This can get pretty hairy.) Another variation of this keeps the original ante card(s) out of play for that game.

## Ante for Set or Match

Agree to play several games, and put aside a single ante for the entire contest. The ante could be just two cards, or it could be proportional to the number of games you will play.

Playing several games rewards the good player instead of the lucky draw.

## Ante for Trade

Instead of taking the entire ante, the winner of the game may choose only one of the cards, giving the loser the other.

## Ante for Show

The cards are laid aside as usual, but the players keep their own cards at the end of the game. This is just to simulate the wager of one card, with nothing really at stake. This handicaps decks which rely on a single card to win.

## Mystery Ante

Ante the cards face down. This adds an element of surprise to the game, so you can win some unknown treasure. You also won't know which card is missing from your deck, so you don't know whether or not your only Disintegrate is still available to cast.

## Overkill Ante

This is a variant for players who believe in taking big risks. At the end of the game, the winner takes one extra, randomly chosen card for each point of damage the loser takes below zero. For example, if you win by doing six points of damage to an opponent with only one life point left, you win a total of five cards from his deck. This may result in odd strategies, such as players holding back on the final kill, waiting to do a 30-point fireball.

# Opening & Draw Variants

## Three Initial Lands

Many players are frustrated by land deficits, especially at the beginning of the game. This variation, designed to make the game more playable for children, allows you to choose any three lands from your deck as part of your starting hand. You then shuffle and draw four more cards to begin.

## Land Stack

This is another beginner's variant: shuffle your lands and spells separately, and draw from either pile as you wish. You may split your opening draw between stacks, but thenceforth, whenever you are required to draw cards, you must choose either one stack or the other. In other words, if a spell makes you draw five cards, you must draw either five lands or five spells.

## No-Land Mulligan, All-Land Mulligan

If you draw no land in the first eight cards, you may declare a misdeal and reshuffle your deck. Alternately, if you draw nothing but land initially, you may request a redeal. In either case, your opponent may elect to redeal his or her own hand.

## Speed Play

Every turn, you draw two cards and immediately discard one of them. You can begin this game as usual, with a starting hand of seven cards, or by drawing fourteen and discarding half of them. Another way to begin this game is to create your opening hand one draw at a time, i.e., drawing two cards and discarding one card, seven times.

## Card Restrictions

If you find that having a minimum of forty cards gives your opponent an unfairly streamlined deck, try increasing the minimum deck size. Wizards of the Coast-sponsored **Magic** tournaments usually enforce a minimum deck size of sixty cards. They also regulate deck composition by holding players to a maximum of four of any spell card except basic land (or, for certain cards, no more than one).

## Burly Wizards

If you prefer a longer game, or have decks that develop more slowly, try starting both players with life totals of 25, 30, or more.

## Turnabout

After a few games, switch decks with your opponent. Play the same number of games again, and see who can get a better game with the same deck. You may also decide to strip out some cards from the switched decks to see who has more skill at deck tuning.

# Other Two-Player Variations

## False Enchantments

You may travel to a place in Dominia where the laws of nature are different. Before the start of the game, agree on an enchantment that will be a permanent game rule. For example, you might choose to have a permanent Mana Flare effect, where all lands produce two mana. The False Enchantment is not treated as an active card in the game—

upkeep is not paid on it, it has no color, and you can't destroy it, modify it, or protect yourself against it, even with Circles of Protection. If you have a copy of that enchantment handy, you might want to lay it out where both players can remember its effects. Also, make sure that the "False Enchantment" affects both players equally—try to avoid using things such as a permanent Karma unless both players are using swamps.

Some other cards have ongoing effects just like enchantments; you might try using them instead. If the card says "you," or "your opponent," assume it refers to both players.

## Two Players, One Deck

If you only have one deck of **Magic** cards, you can see how well it does against itself. Both players share one library and one graveyard. This means that you can kill your opponent's Craw Wurm and resurrect it yourself!

## Two Players, One Hand

Again, players share one library and one graveyard. Deal a hand of seven cards faceup in the middle of the playing area. Both players may use lands and spells from this pool of cards. Once your opponent has cast a spell out of the hand, you no longer have any control over it. For example, only the one who casts Lich forfeits any life points, and if you play a Black Vise, only your opponent will take damage from it.

The strategies in this variant are bizarre. You will find that it often helps to cast spells for no reason, just to prevent your opponent from using them. If you must discard, you'll throw away the card that your opponent needs most.

# Bullseye

You must reduce your opponent to exactly zero life points. Damage done to you by your opponent in excess of the required amount is added back onto your life total. If you were at three life points and sustained ten points of damage at once, you would emerge with seven life points. All creature damage from a single attack is treated as simultaneous damage.

However, spells and other cards in your control do not give you life in this manner. You may not Fireball yourself back up to seven points, though your opponent can Fireball you, increasing your life points, and then attack to bring you down to zero.

## Shoot the Moon

If a player can manage to lose all life in the first four rounds, he wins. Channel, Lich, and other "throw-away-life" effects are not allowed during the first four rounds, although Fireballing yourself is permitted. This variation keeps people from doing a quick kill, and lets slower decks evolve before the battle begins.

# Solitaire Variants

It is difficult to come up with a one-player version of **Magic**. For one thing, it's hard to convert the basic objective—reduce your opponent's life points to zero—into a one-player scenario. For another thing, if you know the rules of the game and you know who you'll be playing against (yourself), it's not difficult to tune a deck that will win every time. It's generally accepted that if you want an enjoyable and challenging solitaire game, you can't allow yourself to tune a deck specifically for it. Instead, play with a deck you use for two-player **Magic**, or start with an unaltered Starter Deck.

There have been some ridiculous attempts at single player **Magic**, including simply drawing two creatures to see if the first one can kill the second. There are, however, a couple of fairly playable solitaire games.

# Wipeout

You have seven turns in which to do yourself 20 points of damage. You may not count mana burn, Channel, Lich, or other "throw-away-life" effects towards this total. You may, however, attack yourself with creatures, and use spells, artifacts, and enchantments originally intended for use against your opponent.

# Demolition

Try to empty your hand and have no cards left in play. If you run out of cards, or take 20 points of damage, you lose. You may not discard from your hand. Your creatures may attack each other. Lands and other permanent cards can be destroyed using the appropriate spells. You may also destroy any card in play by paying its casting cost in life points. Lands may be discarded from play at a rate of one per turn, at no cost in life points; additional lands may be removed at a cost of 8 life points each.

# Multiplayer Variations

Besides team play, which involves two groups engaged in a single battle, there are other ways for more than two people to play **Magic**.

## Three-Way Magic

### Free-For-All

Each player starts with 20 life points and attempts to reduce everyone else down to zero. You need to decide beforehand whether or not a player can divide an attack between both opponents, or if one player may only attack one player at a time. In this, as in most of the other multiplayer games described below, cards which affect "your opponent" affect both of the other players. When one player is eliminated from the game, that player's cards are removed from play, and the game reverts to standard two-player rules.

### Attack to the Left

One of the main problems in a free-for-all is that players tend to pick on the loser. It makes sense to try to get rid of the easiest target first. In this variation, players may only attack (with creatures) the player to their left. Spells may be cast on either player as usual. If you destroy the player to your left, you win.

### Cutthroat

When it's your turn in Cutthroat, the other two players are united against you. This means that their defenses are joined, so that if one of them blocks your attack, it damages neither of them. It also means that their life totals are locked, so if you damage them, you are doing an equal amount to both players. For example, if you cast a Lightning Bolt on your turn, each of your opponents will take 3 points of damage. If you attack with a Craw Wurm (6/4 creature) and one of them uses a Forcefield (take only 1 damage from an unblocked creature,) then they each take only 1 point of damage. If the Wurm isn't stopped, they each suffer 6 points.

If, during your turn, your opponents affect their own life totals, they also affect each other's. If one of them uses a Soul Net, they both gain a life. If one of the casts a Lightning Bolt on the other, they both take 3 points of damage. The one exception to this "joined players" rule is in the mana pool. Defenders may never share or exchange mana points, nor will one defender be burned if the other taps too much mana.

Damage you sustain on your turn is treated normally and not shared with anyone.

When one of the players is eliminated, this becomes a basic two-player game.

## Negative points

This is a variation which can be used with Cutthroat, Free-For-All, and some other multiplayer variations. The object of the game is to drive everyone else below zero life points. Players with less than zero life remain in the game until only one player remains above zero. Players with negative life totals keep track of them just like ordinary life points; for example, players with life point values below zero may still cast spells like Stream of Life which bring them back to positive life points.

The negative-points rule was created to preserve the integrity of certain multiplayer schemes that only work properly when all of the players are still in the game. It also eliminates the nuisance of removing permanent spells cast by a just-eliminated player.

## Five-Way and More

### Five-way Free-For-All

This is another basic pick-on-the-loser game. Players may only attack (with creatures) the players on their immediate left and right, but may affect any player (or any player's cards) with spells. Global effects affect all five players, or all four opponents, whichever is appropriate.

### Limited Range, Attack Left

This version may be played with any number of participants. Players have a limited area of effect—they may only attack to their immediate left, and may cast spells with a maximum range of two players in either direction. With more than eight or nine players, it helps speed up the game to have more than one turn happening at once, since players at opposite sides of the table cannot affect each other. Score one point each time the player on your left is eliminated, and score one and a half points for being the last survivor. The highest score wins.

## Rainbow Magic

In this five-player variant, each player represents one of the colors of **Magic**, playing an appropriate single-color deck. Players sit in a circle in the order depicted on the back of the **Magic** cards. The winner of this game is the magician who eliminates both of the players seated opposite him.

There are several optional ingredients to this five-player **Magic** game:

**Disallow certain cards:** Cards like Karma, Flashfires, and other anti-color cards are much more effective when you are positive that your opponent will be playing those affected colors. If you find that any of these cards consistently slants the game in one person's favor, you may wish to restrict or prohibit that card. In theory, if every player has equal access to the appropriate color-specific cards, the game will be fair without these restrictions.

**Negative points:** Players with negative life points stay in the game. When two neighbors are below zero, the player opposite them is the winner, unless he also has less than zero points. (See **Three-Player Magic** Negative Points variation, above.)

**Star-shaped progression:** Instead of moving around the circle (Green–White–Blue–Black–Red), the turn progresses in a star shape (White–Black–Green–Blue–Red.) This lets enemies move directly after one another.

**Attack Your Enemies:** You may only attack (with creatures) those two players whom you are trying to destroy. For example, White's armies may only attack those of Red and Black. However, for purposes of directed spells, players may still pick appropriate targets from the entire table. Also, "your opponent" still includes all four other players.

**Defending *en passant*:** With a Star-Shaped turn progression, and Attack Your Enemies rules, an attacking creature may be blocked by a creature controlled by the magician whose territory lies between the attacker and the defender. This defense is *en passant*, and taps the defending creature. For example, White attacks Black with a Pearled Unicorn. Black declares a defense. Blue may also, at this time, declare a defense *en passant*, tapping her Phantom Monster to block the Unicorn before it arrives in Black's territory. This adds additional steps and a bit more complexity to the attack, so be sure that all the players understand this variation in the same way before you play with it.

**Cutthroat rules:** As in three-way Cutthroat, when it's your turn, the two players opposite you are united as one. When it's White's turn, Black and Red work together against her.

# Building a *Magic: The Gathering* League

*Joel Mick*

One of Richard Garfield's primary goals for *Magic: The Gathering* was to provide a game that could be enjoyed by large groups of players. This section details a league structure that provides ways for large groups to play **Magic** in an organized, competitive fashion.

## Basic Structure

A league should have at least four players and no more than eight or ten, depending on your level and style of play. League play usually begins with a draft, consisting of a series of rounds in which players take turns selecting cards from a card pool assembled by the league. After the draft, players may be given a period in which to make trades and play preseason games. When this period is over, each participant plays a fixed number of duels against each other player. The player with the best overall record wins the league championship.

## Advantages

League play is one of the most challenging ways to play **Magic**. Although luck of the draw will always be an element of the game, league play emphasizes skill by giving all players the same ability to draft a powerful and versatile deck. Also, because the cards available for play are limited to the initial draft pool, league play encourages players to develop new and interesting uses for less powerful cards that they might not have played with outside of the league. Finally, because each player knows the rough composition of his opponent's deck prior to the duel, the play of the cards often involves additional strategy that is absent or minimized in other forms of **Magic**. For example, a player may know that his opponent has drafted Wrath of God, a spell that destroys all creatures in play. He then must decide whether to summon all of his creatures as quickly as possible, trying for a quick kill, or to hold some creatures in his hand, attempting to whittle down his opponent's life points while ensuring that Wrath of God will not spell certain defeat.

# Organization

## Commisioners

One player should be selected as league commissioner and a second player should be selected as assistant commissioner. The league commissioner is responsible for arbitrating all disputes that arise in the league, including disputes over the function of the **Magic** cards themselves. However, if a dispute involves the league commissioner, then the assistant commissioner should make the required ruling. If both commissioners are involved, the matter should be settled by a majority vote of all players in the league. Generally, the commissioners should be the most experienced **Magic** players or should have previous experience as commissioner in a Rotisserie™ or Strat-o-matic™ Baseball league, or other similar league.

# Draft organizer and statistician

Your **Magic** league will also need a draft organizer and a statistician. The draft organizer is responsible for making sure that all players know what cards are available for the draft, deciding exactly how the draft will be run, and arranging a time and place for the players to get together for the draft.

The statistician is responsible for keeping track of the **Magic** league results. These tasks should not be very time consuming, so the same person could easily serve as commissioner, draft organizer, and statistician.

# The Draft

## Pool Size

The initial drafting pool should have at least sixty cards per player. Since the minimum size of a deck is forty cards, giving each player sixty cards allows plenty of room to trade several cards for one. It also gives players enough flexibility to select cards like the Circles of Protection, which are very powerful against some opponents but not as useful against others.

## Card List

The draft organizer should begin by separating the initial draft pool into lands and spells, and into the different colors of magic. The organizer should provide a complete list of available cards to the other players well in advance of the draft date so that the players can plan their drafting strategies. Unless everyone in the league is extremely knowledgeable about **Magic**, this list should also include a brief explanation of each card's effect. The cards should also be marked in some way to prevent them from getting mixed up with the players' other cards. Although any method of marking that distinguishes the cards will work, placing colored stickers somewhere on the face of each card is recommended because it does not permanently deface the cards and it keeps the backs of the cards looking identical so players cannot guess what card is coming up next.

## Draft Order

The draft organizer is also responsible for determining the drafting order for each round. To prevent one player from having the advantage of drafting first in every round, the drafting order should shift each round. For example, in a six-player league, the drafting order for the first six rounds might be:

| Round 1: | 1–2–3–4–5–6 |
| Round 2: | 2–3–4–5–6–1 |
| Round 3: | 3–4–5–6–1–2 |
| Round 4: | 4–5–6–1–2–3 |
| Round 5: | 5–6–1–2–3–4 |
| Round 6: | 6–1–2–3–4–5 |

Rounds 7–12 could then repeat the drafting order from rounds 1–6, and so on. This order is quite advantageous for player 3, who gets early picks in the first three rounds, and is most disadvantageous for player 6. An alternative drafting order that eliminates this inequity could have the players draft as follows:

| Round 1: | 1–2–3–4–5–6 |
| Round 2: | 6–5–4–3–2–1 |

Subsequent rounds would then repeat this cycle. Although this drafting order appears more equitable, it does permit players 1 and 6 to draft two cards consecutively each cycle, which has been found to be a sizeable advantage. Of course there are a tremendous number of possible draft orders, so the draft organizer could create a few possibilities and try to get a consensus among the players as to which is most fair.

After the draft organizer has determined the drafting order, each player in the league should be assigned a different random number (between one and six in the case of a six player league) to establish where he drafts in each round. The easiest way to assign numbers is to take playing cards (ace through six in the case of a six-player league) and deal one card to each player.

## Draft Divisions

Although it is recommended that a **Magic** league have no more than eight players, larger groups can be accommodated by separating the players into two or more divisions for the drafting phase. Drafts with more than eight players tend to be extremely slow, especially if some of the players are not familiar with all of the available cards.

# Trading and Preseason Games

## Trade Restrictions

It is strongly recommended that trading be prohibited once the regular season begins. Without a trading prohibition, a player with a deck consisting of mostly red magic might play her first matches against the player who had drafted the only Circle of Protection: Red. Another player might then trade for this card, and the player with the red magic deck would be forced to play a second set of matches against this card. This situation is not only unfair—it also encourages the player with the red magic deck to postpone her duels against the player with the Circle of Protection: Red until last.

## Preseason Games

After the draft, many players will be eager to play with their new decks. Others may feel that they still have significant trading to do before they have optimized their decks. Because no trading is allowed once the regular season begins, some time period, from as little as a few hours to as much as a few weeks, should be dedicated to the preseason to accommodate the different desires of the players. During the preseason, all duels are strictly for fun— no ante is permitted, and the duels do not count toward the players' final records. Trading is totally unrestricted during the preseason, although less experienced players should always ask a disinterested player's advice before agreeing to a trade.

# Regular Season Games

## Structure of Competition

The regular season is composed of a series of matches. Generally, each player will play two matches against each other player, each match consisting of a number of duels. Two matches allows each player to be the "home" team in one match against a particular opponent and the "visiting" team in the other match. Being the visiting team means nothing more than getting to take the first turn in the first duel of that match, with the loser of each duel going first in the following duel. In a six-player league, for example, each player might play two five-duel matches against each of the other five players, for a total of fifty duels per player. The total number of duels each player will have can be adjusted easily by changing the number of duels per match or number of matches per season. Just make sure that the total number of duels is large enough so that skill will predominate, but small enough so that players don't get tired of playing so many games with the same deck.

## Playing Without Ante

It is recommended that regular season matches not be played for ante. One problem with playing for ante is that a player who gets unlucky and loses a few of his most powerful cards in early matches will have little chance of recovering by getting equally lucky later, since his deck will now be weaker. Also, assuming that trading is prohibited during the regular season, players will often win cards that they cannot reasonably play with. (If you do choose to play a league with ante, you may wish to permit trading but limit it to letting a player trade back a card just won to its former owner.) Finally, playing for ante gives players an incentive to play their matches in a particular order. Players will prefer to play weaker opponents first, hoping to win cards that will help them against more powerful opponents later. Without ante, players can be permitted to play each other in any order, at their mutual convenience. This will cause the league to run much faster and more smoothly.

## Card Selection

Before each match, both players should secretly select the cards that will form their deck for that match from all of their league cards. While a player's deck must have a minimum of forty cards, she need not play with all of her cards, and may choose never to play with some of them. Once a player has formed her deck, she is not permitted to add or remove cards from it at any time during a match. Thus there can be significant strategy in predicting what cards your opponent is likely to play with and selecting your cards to combat them most effectively. There will also be additional strategy in the first few games as you discover which cards your opponent has chosen to play with and which have been left out.

## League Results

When a match is completed, one player should report the results to the league statistician. The statistician will keep track of each player's record and how many games each player has left. The statistician should periodically report the current standings to the other players. You should decide before starting the league whether you want playoff matches between the players with the best records. If so, you must also decide whether you only want one match between the top two players or some other form of playoff. However, you may choose to forego playoffs altogether. Many players believe that the league should reward the player who has the most versatile deck, the one that works best against all the other decks in the league. Having playoffs means that the player with the best overall record may lose to someone whose deck just happens to match up especially well against hers.

## Variations

### Card Selection

These rules describe only one of many methods for operating a **Magic** league. Every aspect of league play has innumerable variations. There are, for example, numerous alternatives to the drafting method presented above. One alternative would be to replace the round system with a bidding system. Each player would begin with a number of points, perhaps 250. Players would then take turns nominating cards, accompanied by an initial bid. All players would then be permitted to increase the bid on the nominated card, with the player submitting the highest bid ultimately receiving the card and having his bid subtracted from his available points. Because this process is slower than drafting by rounds, and because the difference in strength between many of the less powerful cards is not great, a hybrid structure with bidding on the first 20 percent of cards and drafting by rounds thereafter might work best.

## Preexisting Decks

Another alternative to the round structure would be to allow players to create their league decks out of **Magic** cards that they already own. Some constraint would need to be placed on deck composition to prevent the players who own the most cards from having an insurmountable advantage. For example, players might be limited to no more than two of any individual common card, and no more than one of any individual uncommon or rare card, with an additional limitation of ten total uncommon cards and three total rare cards per deck. To make the league more equitable, players owning fewer cards might be permitted to borrow cards from other players for use in the league.

## Duplicate Magic

There are also a number of variations to the scheduling of games. For example, the league could be run like a duplicate bridge tournament, with each player taking a turn dueling with each deck against each other deck. In a six-player league, each player would need to play 30 duels in order to play one duel with each of the six decks against each of the five others. A 90-duel schedule could be devised whereby each player plays three duels with each deck against each other deck, with each player engaging in 18 total duels against each other player. This variation would eliminate the value of deck composition skills, and would reward the player who is most skillful at playing the available cards. The decks used for this league variation need not be drafted, but could rather be contributed by the players or set up by the commissioner. In order for this duplicate league to be successful, the decks should be of approximately equal power.

# Rotisserie™ Magic

A **Magic** league could also be run like a Rotisserie™ Baseball league, with the cards divided into one-season, two-season, and three-season categories. Players would draft cards, trade, and play a full set of matches. After that season was over, all of the one-season cards would be removed from the league, the two-season cards would become one-season cards, the three-season cards would become two-season cards, and a miniature draft would take place to replace the cards removed from the league. Cards from this miniature draft would become three-season cards, and the next season would be played. In such a Rotisserie-style league, players could trade away powerful two- or three-season cards for more powerful one-season cards in an attempt to win the current season. However, they would suffer in the following seasons as a result of the trade. Such a scheme thus gives everyone, including the less skillful players, a good chance to be at the top of the league for a season.

## Handicaps

Finally: If your **Magic** league contains both beginners and experts, you may wish to give the beginners some form of handicap. This handicap could take the form of a draft preference, such as switching some of the beginners' later round picks with the experts' earlier round picks, or giving the beginners extra points to bid with in a bidding draft. Beginners could also be given a handicap in the play of the duels. For example, when a beginner plays an expert, the beginner might be permitted to go first every duel, or to start with 25 life points. The expert could even be required to start each duel with six cards instead of seven, although starting with fewer cards has been found to be a tremendous disadvantage.

# Team Magic

*Jim Lin*

## Introduction

While **Magic** was originally designed as a one-on-one duel, many people have found that playing **Magic** in teams can add new and refreshing elements to the game. For one thing, teams make it easier for players of differing power to have fun together. In most play groups, you invariably end up with a few people with killer decks and a few people with weak decks. It's not very much fun for either side when one player always wins by turn four, while her opponent would be happy merely to deal a point or two of damage by turn four. One way to solve this problem is to play in teams with the strong players divided between the teams.

If you have never played team **Magic** before, be ready to be pleasantly surprised. You will find that there are a lot of new strategies, and many of your old strategies won't work anymore. In team **Magic**, the relative power of the cards can differ dramatically from the two-player game. For example, a deck that features Channel and Disintegrate is pretty fearsome in a one-on-one duel. Starting on turn three or so, your opponent has to worry that you are about to channel all but one of your life points away and kill them in one fell swoop. In team play, however, this strategy isn't all that exciting. You may kill one player, but when his partner kills you the next turn it's back to an even match.

On the other hand, experience has shown that the life-giving artifacts, such as Wooden Sphere, aren't always that useful in normal games of **Magic**. There simply aren't enough spells of the right kind played for you to get a significant amount of life. In larger games of **Magic**, however, particularly three-on-three, you can build up a sizable lead from these artifacts.

When you are playing team versions, feel free to experiment. The guidelines given below are rules that work well, but there are any number of other structures you could use.

## Basic Mechanics

Most of the rules that govern two-player **Magic** also apply in a team game. All players still start out with 20 life points, and the goal is to kill all of the players on the opposing side. One interesting possibility is to designate one player as the "emperor" of each side. It then becomes the goal of each team to kill the opposing emperor. In general, the process of drawing cards, playing lands and casting spells does not change in team **Magic**—the few exceptions are noted below.

## Choosing Sides and the Number of Players

The first thing you need to decide is the number of players. Four-player games (two-on-two) and six-player games (three-on-three) work extremely well, while games involving more players tend to drag on. If you have only one person with a really nasty deck, however, it is possible to handicap the side that player is on. Be careful when doing this, though, as having more players on your side is an extremely large advantage. In many team games, when one team kills one of the opposing players, the effect snowballs, and the game ends quickly. Three-on-two can be made to work reasonably well, but if you intend to play two-on-one, the player that is being double-teamed had better have a ridiculously powerful deck. If all of the players are of roughly equal strength, a simple way to choose sides is to shuffle up two sets of lands and have the players draw. All of the players that draw one type of land are on a team.

## Seating Arrangement

There are several interesting ways to set up a team game. One method is to seat the players in a circle, alternating between teams, so that each player sits between two of their opponents. Play moves in a clockwise fashion. When a player is killed, his turn is skipped when it comes around. This format is recommended for playing two-on-two games.

The other seating arrangement can be best explained as having each team sitting on one side of a table, in a line. Since turns still pass in a clockwise fashion, this results in all of the players on one team taking a turn, and then all of the players on the other team taking a turn. This method is recommended for playing three-on-three games. Note that this results in one player on each side who is not adjacent to an opponent. This person in the center is often referred to as the "general" or "emperor."

## Card Range and Effects

One of the most important aspects of team **Magic** is deciding how to limit where and when you can use your cards. While it may seem natural that you should be able to summon creatures and place them in front of your teammates, team **Magic** works better when the restrictions on playing cards are more stringent. The following set of rules are recommended.

## Cards Affecting You

Cards such as summonings, artifacts, and blanket enchantments (that is, enchantments that don't enchant something specific) can only be played in front of you. Thus, you can't play a Circle of Protection: Red to protect your teammate from those annoying Lightning Bolts. Any card that specifies "yours" or "controller's" can still only be played on something you control. Even if your partner is willing, you can't sacrifice your partner's creatures. Similarly, any card that affects only you or something of yours still doesn't affect your partners or any of their cards—your Orcish Oriflamme makes your creatures +1/+0 when they attack, but not your partners'.

## Cards Affecting Other Players

Any card that requires or allows you to affect something of your "opponent's" may be played on *any* player besides yourself, including your partners. Thus, you may use Ancestral Recall to cause one of your partners to draw three cards. Similarly, any card with effects that influence your "opponent" is considered to affect *all* players other than you. Thus, Black Vise would deal damage to all of your opponents and all of your partners if they had more than four cards in their hand during upkeep. Also, any cards that affect "all" of something affect both teams.

## Cards Affecting Any Player

Any card that does not specifically state that you must play it on yourself or your opponent can be played on any player. Thus, you can use Lightning Bolt to do 3 points of damage to any player or any creature in play, including your partners or their creatures.

## Side Rules

Sometimes it is desirable to allow a few exceptions to the rules given above. For example, Lifetap might be too powerful, since it means that you gain life when your partners tap their forests. The intention of Lifetap is to punish your opponents for playing with green magic, not to reward your partners for doing so. Similarly, you might decide that Black Vise isn't intended to punish your friends, just your enemies. If everyone agrees to it, you may make a side rule that Black Vise only works on your opponents, not your partners. If there is some dispute or disagreement, however, the default rules should be used. Make sure that everyone playing agrees to any side rules ahead of time. In general, these rules should only reduce the strength of specific cards, not increase the strength of weak cards.

# Attacking

This is the most complicated aspect of team play, and the area where the most new strategy and forethought is required.( This is particularly true in three-on-three games where the teams are arrayed in a line.) However, the unusual dynamics of creature combat in team **Magic** can be extremely rewarding.

## Moving Creatures

The most important combat difference between one-on-one and team **Magic** lies in the position and capabilities of creatures that you control and with which you can attack. In team **Magic**, you can't directly summon a creature in front of your teammate, but you can move your creatures from your territory into the territory of one of your teammates. You still maintain control over that creature, and only you can choose to attack with it, but only during your own attack phase.

## Rules for Creature Movement

Moving a creature from your territory to a teammate's territory is considered to be the equivalent of an attack. Thus, a creature may not move and then attack. However, when you move a creature from your own territory, the creature is not tapped in the process. Creatures that are currently tapped and walls may not be moved. A creature can only be moved once per turn, and it may not be moved on the turn it is summoned.

## Range of Creature Movement: Line Seating

If you started off the game in a line format, you may move creatures from your territory to that of any teammate you are sitting next to. Thus, in a three-on-three game, creatures in front of the players at the end of the lines may only be moved to in front of the general. Creatures in front of the general may move to either of the general's teammates' territory.

## Range of Creature Movement: Circular Seating

If you started off the game in a circle, then creatures may move from one player's territory to that of any teammate that is two people away or less. In two-on-two or three-on-three versions of the game, this means that creatures may always move from any teammate to any other teammate, but if you play a circular seating game with four players on a side, creatures in front of you will not be able to move from your territory to the territory of the player directly opposite you on your team until some of your opponents or teammates in between are eliminated.

## Attack Range

Creatures in front of a player may only attack opponents that are sitting next to that player. This means that in circular two-on-two **Magic**, creatures in front of you may attack either of your opponents. Creatures that are in front of the "general" in three-on-three **Magic** (if you are sitting in the recommended line setup) are not initially allowed to attack any of the opponents. When a player is eliminated, however, play continues as if that player did not exist. This can drastically affect what creatures in front of you may do. You may suddenly go from being in a position where no creatures could attack you to one where many creatures are attacking you. Of course, that also means that creatures in front of you would have something to attack, too. If you kill both of the opponents next to you in the circle, the creatures in front of you will not be able to attack until one of your teammates is eliminated.

## Control of Moved Creatures

Be careful to remember that the person who is controlling the creature is not changed by the creature's current location. Thus, if you move one of your creatures in front of one of your teammates, that creature still belongs to you. It attacks when the rest of your creatures attack, it only blocks attackers if you say it does, and it untaps at the same time all of your creatures untap. This may result in several waves of creatures attacking from the same player's territory as different players take their turn. A creature can only be moved on its controller's turn; thus, your partner cannot move any of the creatures you control during her turn, whether or not they are in her territory.

## Attacking with Moved Creatures

A player may attack more than one opponent during a single attack phase. This means that during your attack phase, any of your creatures, including creatures that are in front of your teammates but still under your control, may attack as long as they all attack opponents that are adjacent to the players they are in front of.

## Defending with Moved Creatures

When you are attacked by another player's creatures, any of the creatures in front of you may be used to block attacking creatures. Remember, however, that you do not always control all of the creatures in front of you. Some may belong to your teammates, and they still make the decisions for those creatures. If several players' creatures are defending against the same attack, the players make all the decisions about the blocking in order, clockwise, starting with the player who is being attacked.

## Forced Attacks

If a creature is forced to attack by some effect, the creature must attack an opponent if it is in front of a player who is adjacent to an opponent. If the player is adjacent to two opponents, the controller of the creature forced to attack may choose which opponent the creature attacks. If the creature is in front of a player who is not sitting next to an opponent, then the controller of the creature must move the creature so that it is in front of another partner. If it is possible to move the creature to be in front of a partner who is adjacent to an opponent, that move must be chosen.

# Communication

The last issue to resolve before playing a game of team **Magic** is how much teams can communicate. If the teammates are allowed to show each other their hands, talk about any moves they want to make, and so on, team games can drag on and on. On the other hand, trying to coordinate maneuvers between teammates while having limited communications can be an enjoyable challenge.

While you are still learning the ropes of team **Magic**, it is probably easier to relax the restrictions on communications a little bit. One option that works well, if it is not abused, is to allow players to give suggestions about any card in play or ask for suggestions about any card in play. They may still not mention anything about what is in their hands. For example, you could specifically request that your partner block with one of his creatures. However, if you wanted your partner to block because you were planning to use Giant Growth or some other spell to help in the combat, you may not mention that. Obviously, this restriction is a little vague, and requires a group of players who are willing to abide by the spirit as well as the letter of the rules.

Once you have some experience in playing team **Magic**, you might require that the partners not be allowed to communicate at all, with the one exception that when players are attacked, they can ask the owner of any untapped creature in front of them whether the owner intends to block with that creature or not. If more than one of the player's partners controls creatures in front of them, they may choose in which order to ask the partners whether they are going to block with their creatures or not. Note that players are still not allowed to advise their partners whether they want the creatures to block.

These systems for seating, card effects, and communication can and should change as your team games evolve. If the members of your playgroup find that these guidelines become cumbersome, they should experiment with other adaptations to the rules. After all, there are as many interesting ways to play **Magic** as there are players. Team **Magic** provides a perfect forum for many different players to develop and enjoy these innovations together.

# Duelists' Convocation Magic Tournament Rules

Please note that these rules are frequently modified in order to support the latest expansions and changes in the *Magic: The Gathering—Revised Edition*. The version of the tournament rules presented here supports the initial Limited Edition cards, the Unlimited Edition and Revised Edition cards, and the *Arabian Nights* expansion set. Updated rules are provided at officially sanctioned *Magic: The Gathering* tournaments.

## Deck Construction Rules

1.  The tournament deck must contain a minimum of 60 cards, total, inclusive of all lands, creatures, spells, and artifacts. This helps to ensure more variety in play, thus testing the players' skill to a greater degree. In addition to the tournament deck, players may construct a Sideboard of exactly 15 additional cards. Players are not required to use a Sideboard, but if they do, it must always contain exactly 15 cards. The use of the Sideboard will be further explained under Floor Rules (Rule #5).

2.  There may be no more than 4 of any individual card in the tournament deck (including Sideboard), with the exception of the five basic land types (Plains, Forest, Mountain, Island, Swamp). This rule expands the variety of spells and creatures that will be encountered during play, giving players the opportunity to utilize more combinations of effects.

3.  The Deck Construction Rules also include what is called the Restricted List. For each of the cards on

the Restricted List, no more than one may ever be drawn from a player's library, or brought into a game from outside (such as with a Ring of Ma'Ruf) during the course of a duel. If more than one is drawn from the library or brought into the game, the second card is called a "Restricted List duplicate." As will be explained in the Floor Rules, at the end of every duel each player will check his opponent's graveyard, cards in play, cards left in his hand, and any cards that were "removed entirely from game." If any Restricted List duplicates are found in any of these areas, the offending player will immediately forfeit that match. The Restricted List serves to limit those cards that, in certain combinations with other cards, create situations that disturb game balance. A further explanation of how this rule is applied can be found under Floor Rules (Rule #8). The Restricted List may be modified at any time to include future card releases, or at any other time, by the Director of the Duelists' Convocation (see Floor Rules, Rule #11). The current Restricted List includes these cards from *Magic: The Gathering* and *Magic: The Gathering—Arabian Nights*:

Ali from Cairo
Ancestral Recall
Berserk
Black Lotus
Brain Geyser
Channel
Copy Artifact
Demonic Tutor
Dingus Egg
Gauntlet of Might
Mox Pearl

Mox Emerald
Mox Ruby
Mox Sapphire
Mox Jet
Regrowth
Sol Ring
Timetwister
Time Walk
Wheel of Fortune

4. The following cards are banned from official tournament decks:
   Contract from Below
   Darkpact
   Demonic Attorney
   Jeweled Bird
   Shahrazad
   Time Vault

   The first four cards in the list are not allowed because they clearly state to remove them from your deck if not playing for ante, and ante is not required to be wagered in an official tournament (see Floor Rules, Rule #6). Any future cards that make the same statement will also be banned. Shahrazad requires players to play sub-games of **Magic**; this simply takes too long and holds up the whole tournament. The last card on the list can drastically unbalance game play by allowing a player to cycle through his deck quickly.

5. Decks may be constructed from cards from the Limited (black border) series and from the Unlimited or Revised (white border) series. Use of cards from any of the expansion sets (i.e., *Arabian Nights*, etc.) are permitted with the Referee's prior consent. Under no circumstances will cards from the Collectors' Edition sets be permitted in tournament decks. They are easily distinguished from tournament-legal cards by their square corners and gold trim, as well as the text "Collectors' Edition" on the card backs. Use of Collectors' Edition set cards in a tournament deck will be interpreted by the Judge as a Declaration of Forfeiture (see Floor Rules, Rule #10).

# Floor Rules

1. Tournaments will use a standard ladder-bracket system. Single or double elimination tournaments are both acceptable. A ladder chart should be prepared with players' names and Duelists' Convocation membership numbers clearly printed in their ladder positions. The players should be allowed to view the chart at any time between their matches, at their request.

2. The total number of players in the tournament should be an even factor of two (i.e., 16, 32, 64, etc.) This is to avoid the problem of assigning byes during a tournament in which individual rounds will most likely not be concluded simultaneously. Byes can be assigned, however, and should be used (if necessary).

3. Tournaments will be presided over by a Judge, who may be assisted by as many Assistant Referees as needed. A Judge may be required to interpret rules, to terminate an excessively long match, to interpret a Declaration of Forfeiture, or make any other adjudication as necessary during the tournament. The Judge is also responsible for maintaining the ladder chart, and only the Judge is permitted to write on the chart (i.e., listing advancing players on the bracket). Assistant Referees will aid the Judge by answering rules questions on the floor and being available to the Judge for any other assistance required. Any Referee's decision is final; however, in necessary cases, the Judge may overrule any decision made by an Assistant Referee. The decision of the Judge is always final.

4. A duel is one complete game of **Magic**. A match is defined as the best two out of three duels for standard rounds, and the best three out of five duels for semifinal and final rounds of a tournament. A player may advance in the tournament bracket after successfully winning one match, and reporting this victory to the Judge.

5. Players must use the same deck that they begin the tournament with throughout the duration of the tournament. The only deck alteration permitted is through the use of the Sideboard (see Deck Construction Rules, Rule #1). If a player intends to use a Sideboard during the course of a match, they must declare to their opponent that they will be using the Sideboard prior to the beginning of that match. Players may exchange cards from their deck for cards from their Sideboard on a one-for-one basis at any time between duels or matches. There are no restrictions on how many cards a player may exchange in this way at any given time. Prior to the beginning of any duel, each player must allow his or her opponent to count, face down, the number of cards in his or her Sideboard. If a player's Sideboard does not total exactly 15 cards, the Judge or an Assistant Referee must be consulted to evaluate the situation before the duel can begin. If a player claims that they are not using a Sideboard at the beginning of the match, ignore this counting procedure for that player, but no deck alteration of any kind will be permitted by the Judge for that player for the duration of that match. Any violation of this rule may be interpreted by the Judge as a Declaration of Forfeiture.

6.   Players are not required to wager ante during the tournament. Players will remove a "fake ante" from their deck prior to duels, using the same process as real ante. "Fake ante" is not claimed by the winner; instead, it is returned to the owner's deck at the conclusion of the duel. Players may play for real ante, provided that both participants in the match give their consent.

7.   Players may not have any outside assistance (i.e., coaching) during a match. Players in violation will receive one warning; any further infractions will be interpreted by the Judge as a Declaration of Forfeiture.

8.   At the conclusion of every duel, each player must show the remaining cards in his or her hand to the opponent to verify that no Restricted List duplicate cards appear there (e.g., to prove that a second Time Walk wasn't drawn from his library). Players may then check their opponents' graveyards, playing fields, and areas where players have stored cards that have been "removed entirely from play" during the duel in order to assess that no Restricted List duplicates appear in any of those areas. Once this has been accomplished to both players' satisfaction, the duel can be considered officially finished, with a winner declared. If there are any disagreements between the players, the Judge must be consulted to officially close the duel and declare a winner. If Restricted List duplicates are found, the Judge will enforce the forfeiture of the match by the offending player (see Deck Construction Rules, Rule #3). Note that it is possible for both players to forfeit

the match in this fashion, in which case they will both be removed from the tournament bracket.

9. Players must at all times keep the cards in their hands above the level of the playing surface. If a player is in violation, the Judge may issue a warning to the player, or interpret the violation as a Declaration of Forfeiture.

10. Failure to adhere to the above rules, or any other rules specific to a particular tournament, may be interpreted by the Judge as a Declaration of Forfeiture. This is a more pleasant way of stating that if a player cheats, the Judge will remove them from the tournament.

11. The Director of the Duelists' Convocation reserves the exclusive right to add, delete, alter, transmute, polymorph, switch, color-lace, sleight of mind, magical hack, or in any other way change these rules, in whole or in part, with or without notice, at any time that it is deemed necessary or desirable. This right is nonnegotiable.

## Official Tournament Status

An "official" or "officially sanctioned" **Magic** tournament is one that has met the playing criteria of the Duelists' Convocation, has been registered with the Director of the Convocation at Wizards of the Coast, and has been logged as an officially sanctioned event. These tournaments usually follow a version of the tournament rules outlined above. Ranking points can only be awarded for officially sanctioned play. If you are interested in obtaining offical status for a tournament you are sponsoring, contact the Director of the Duelists' Convocation.

# VI

# Collector's Information

## •Magic: A Collecting History

Victor K. Wertz explains the differences between printings of the cards, from the initial run to the Revised Edition.

## •The *Magic: The Gathering* Card List

Finally, here is a complete list of the cards in the original *Magic: The Gathering* print run, including commonality and changes between the Alpha and Beta versions.

## •A Note On Expansion Sets

A source of new surprises for **Magic** players, expansion sets are an important element of Dominia and your deck.

# Magic: A Collecting History

*Victor K. Wertz*

## *Magic: The Gathering*—Limited Edition

Collectors should realize that the first run of *Magic: The Gathering* was one print run of ten million cards, divided more or less evenly into sixty-card decks and fifteen-card booster packs. However, after the first 2.6 million cards (commonly called Alpha cards) were released on September 20, 1993, Wizards of the Coast (WotC) found some problems, and ordered some corrections for the final 7.3 million cards (often referred to as Beta cards).

## Card Errors and Omissions

Most of the card changes involved typographical errors or miscredited artwork. However, WotC took the opportunity to add in a few cards that were accidentally left out of the first part of the press run. The most notable omission was the Circle of Protection: Black, which therefore exists in lesser numbers than other common cards.

## The Rule Book

Wizards of the Coast also worked to clarify the rules. A fantasy story by Richard Garfield, initially found on pages 4 and 5 of the rulebook, was removed to make room for a brief summary of play. The rulebook was expanded from 36 to 40 pages. Pages 36–38 added a list of commonly asked questions, and an index was placed on page 39. The artist credits were then moved from page 36 to page 40. The revised rulebook was inserted into the decks produced in the second part of the print run.

## Packaging and Card Shape

While the presses were stopped, Carta Mundi also made some changes in the packaging. They improved the process of shrinkwrapping the ten-deck in-store display boxes, and added UPC bar codes to the bottom of the individual deck boxes. Finally, before restarting, Carta Mundi sharpened the dies used to cut the cards, which resulted in a smaller corner radius on the cards in the second part of the print run. These cards were released on October 4, 1993.

## Identifying Alpha and Beta Cards

As a result of these changes, the limited print is commonly thought of as two separate print runs. The collector will be able to identify the first 2.6 million cards by their larger corner radius. The original rulebooks, too, can be easily identified by page count. Unopened decks can be identified by the lack of a UPC code on the bottom. Unopened deck display boxes can be identified by the uneven shrinkwrapping. Unopened booster packs and booster displays, however, don't have any apparent differences between the two parts of the print run.

## *Magic: The Gathering* Collectors' Editions

After the first ten million *Magic: The Gathering* cards were printed, WotC issued ten thousand Collectors' Edition sets of *Magic: The Gathering*. These limited-edition sets contained 363 cards, including at least one of each of the 302 different cards, with multiple land cards making up the difference. These ten thousand sets were sold only in the US and Canada, while five thousand International Collectors' Edition sets were produced for sale overseas. Unlike other **Magic** cards, the Collectors' Edition cards have square corners and the card backs have gold borders. Additionally, they have gold lettering on the back of each card that marks them as either Collectors' Edition or International Edition cards. These took some time to produce, but were finally released on December 10, 1993.

## Magic: The Gathering—Unlimited Edition

Next, Wizards of the Coast instructed Carta Mundi to change the black border on the card faces to white for all additional print runs. The phrase Unlimited Edition was also added to the packaging. This helps maintain the collecting value of the initial limited print run. The Unlimited Edition was released on December 1, 1993.

## Magic: The Gathering—Expansion Sets

Wizards of the Coast periodically augments its *Magic: The Gathering* offerings with additional expansion sets. These generally contain between 50 and 400 cards centered around some theme within Dominia. The first expansion set, *Arabian Nights*, was released on December 17, 1993.

## Magic: The Gathering—Revised Edition

The Revised Edition removes some cards deemed too powerful or too confusing, and adds some cards from existing expansion sets to the standard roster. The rules have changed slightly, and have been clarified considerably. They have the same white border as the Unlimited Edition.

## Counterfeit Cards

In addition to all of these official cards, Wizards of the Coast has learned of the existence of counterfeit cards.

These can usually be identified by their lower quality printing and card stock. Also, many of the counterfeit cards are color copies glued to land cards, and can be identified by the double-layer look seen on the edge of the card. These cards are virtually worthless to most collectors.

## Determining Collecting Values

With the proper information at hand (see below), it's easy to determine the rarity of any given card. However, the collector should note that the rarity of a card doesn't necessarily determine its value. To many players, a more powerful card is more important than a rare card; to many collectors, the condition of a card is of vital importance. Also, some people value cards by a specific artist, and simply aren't interested in other factors.

The following pages provide a complete list of the 302 different cards included in the first, limited print run of *Magic: The Gathering*. In addition to providing all of the card names, the list includes color, spell type, artist, commonality, and some notes of interest for collectors. Card lists and collecting information will also be published regularly in *The Duelist*, the official **Deckmaster** magazine.

# Beta/Unlimited Card Checklist

| | CARD NAME | COLOR |
|---|---|---|
| 1 | Air Elemental | Blue |
| 2 | Ancestral Recall | Blue |
| 3 | Animate Artifact | Blue |
| 4 | Animate Dead | Black |
| 5 | Animate Wall | White |
| 6 | Ankh of Mishra | Artifact |
| 7 | Armageddon | White |
| 8 | Aspect of Wolf | Green |
| 9 | Bad Moon | Black |
| 10 | Badlands | None |
| 11 | Balance | White |
| 12* | Basalt Monolith | Artifact |
| 13 | Bayou | None |
| 14 | Benalish Hero | White |
| 15 | Berserk | Green |
| 16* | Birds of Paradise | Green |
| 17 | Black Knight | Black |
| 18 | Black Lotus | Artifact |
| 19 | Black Vise | Artifact |
| 20 | Black Ward | White |
| 21 | Blaze of Glory | White |
| 22 | Blessing | White |
| 23 | Blue Elemental Blast | Blue |
| 24 | Blue Ward | White |
| 25 | Bog Wraith | Black |
| 26 | Braingeyser | Blue |
| 27 | Burrowing | Red |
| 28 | Camouflage | Green |
| 29 | Castle | White |
| 30 | Celestial Prism | Artifact |
| 31* | Channel | Green |
| 32 | Chaos Orb | Artifact |
| 33 | Chaoslace | Red |
| 34* | Circle of Protection: Black | White |
| 35 | Circle of Protection: Blue | White |
| 36 | Circle of Protection: Green | White |

| TYPE | ARTIST'S NAME | COMMONALITY |
|------|---------------|-------------|
| Creature | Richard Thomas | Uncommon |
| Instant | Mark Poole | Rare |
| Enchantment | Douglas Shuler | Uncommon |
| Enchantment | Anson Maddocks | Uncommon |
| Enchantment | Dan Frazier | Rare |
| Continuous | Amy Weber | Rare |
| Sorcery | Jesper Myrfors | Rare |
| Enchantment | Jeff A. Menges | Rare |
| Enchantment | Jesper Myrfors | Rare |
| Land | Rob Alexander | Rare |
| Sorcery | Mark Poole | Rare |
| Mono | Jesper Myrfors | Uncommon |
| Land | Jesper Myrfors | Rare |
| Creature | Douglas Shuler | Common |
| Instant | Dan Frazier | Uncommon |
| Creature | Mark Poole | Rare |
| Creature | Jeff A. Menges | Uncommon |
| Mono | Christopher Rush | Rare |
| Continuous | Richard Thomas | Uncommon |
| Enchantment | Dan Frazier | Uncommon |
| Instant | Richard Thomas | Rare |
| Enchantment | Julie Baroh | Rare |
| Interrupt | Richard Thomas | Common |
| Enchantment | Dan Frazier | Uncommon |
| Creature | Jeff A. Menges | Uncommon |
| Sorcery | Mark Tedin | Rare |
| Enchantment | Mark Poole | Uncommon |
| Instant | Jesper Myrfors | Uncommon |
| Enchantment | Dameon Willich | Uncommon |
| Mono | Amy Weber | Uncommon |
| Sorcery | Richard Thomas | Uncommon |
| Mono | Mark Tedin | Rare |
| Interrupt | Dameon Willich | Rare |
| Enchantment | Jesper Myrfors | Common |
| Enchantment | Dameon Willich | Common |
| Enchantment | Sandra Everingham | Common |

| | CARD NAME | COLOR |
|---|---|---|
| 37* | Circle of Protection: Red | White |
| 38 | Circle of Protection: White | White |
| 39 | Clockwork Beast | Artifact |
| 40 | Clone | Blue |
| 41 | Cockatrice | Green |
| 42 | Consecrate Land | White |
| 43 | Conservator | Artifact |
| 44 | Contract from Below | Black |
| 45 | Control Magic | Blue |
| 46 | Conversion | White |
| 47 | Copper Tablet | Artifact |
| 48 | Copy Artifact | Blue |
| 49 | Counterspell | Blue |
| 50 | Craw Wurm | Green |
| 51 | Creature Bond | Blue |
| 52 | Crusade | White |
| 53 | Crystal Rod | Artifact |
| 54 | Cursed Land | Black |
| 55* | Cyclopean Tomb | Artifact |
| 56 | Dark Ritual | Black |
| 57 | Darkpact | Black |
| 58* | Death Ward | White |
| 59 | Deathgrip | Black |
| 60 | Deathlace | Black |
| 61 | Demonic Attorney | Black |
| 62* | Demonic Hordes | Black |
| 63 | Demonic Tutor | Black |
| 64 | Dingus Egg | Artifact |
| 65 | Disenchant | White |
| 66 | Disintegrate | Red |
| 67 | Disrupting Scepter | Artifact |
| 68 | Dragon Whelp | Red |
| 69* | Drain Life | Black |
| 70 | Drain Power | Blue |
| 71 | Drudge Skeletons | Black |
| 72 | Dwarven Demolition Team | Red |
| 73 | Dwarven Warriors | Red |
| 74 | Earth Elemental | Red |

| TYPE | ARTIST'S NAME | COMMONALITY |
|------|---------------|-------------|
| Enchantment | Mark Tedin | Common |
| Enchantment | Douglas Shuler | Common |
| Creature | Drew Tucker | Rare |
| Creature | Julie Baroh | Uncommon |
| Creature | Dan Frazier | Rare |
| Enchantment | Jeff A. Menges | Uncommon |
| Mono | Amy Weber | Uncommon |
| Sorcery | Douglas Shuler | Rare |
| Enchantment | Dameon Willich | Uncommon |
| Enchantment | Jesper Myrfors | Uncommon |
| Continuous | Amy Weber | Uncommon |
| Enchantment | Amy Weber | Rare |
| Interrupt | Mark Poole | Uncommon |
| Creature | Daniel Gelon | Common |
| Enchantment | Anson Maddocks | Common |
| Enchantment | Mark Poole | Rare |
| Poly | Amy Weber | Uncommon |
| Enchantment | Jesper Myrfors | Uncommon |
| Mono | Anson Maddocks | Rare |
| Interrupt | Sandra Everingham | Common |
| Sorcery | Quinton Hoover | Rare |
| Instant | Mark Poole | Common |
| Enchantment | Anson Maddocks | Uncommon |
| Interrupt | Sandra Everingham | Rare |
| Sorcery | Daniel Gelon | Rare |
| Creature | Jesper Myrfors | Rare |
| Sorcery | Douglas Shuler | Uncommon |
| Continuous | Dan Frazier | Rare |
| Instant | Amy Weber | Common |
| Sorcery | Anson Maddocks | Common |
| Mono | Dan Frazier | Rare |
| Creature | Amy Weber | Uncommon |
| Sorcery | Douglas Shuler | Common |
| Sorcery | Douglas Shuler | Rare |
| Creature | Sandra Everingham | Common |
| Creature | Kev Brockschmidt | Uncommon |
| Creature | Douglas Shuler | Common |
| Creature | Dan Frazier | Uncommon |

| | CARD NAME | COLOR |
|---|---|---|
| 75 | Earthbind | Red |
| 76 | Earthquake | Red |
| 77* | Elvish Archers | Green |
| 78 | Evil Presence | Black |
| 79 | False Orders | Red |
| 80 | Farmstead | White |
| 81 | Fastbond | Green |
| 82 | Fear | Black |
| 83 | Feedback | Blue |
| 84 | Fire Elemental | Red |
| 85 | Fireball | Red |
| 86 | Firebreathing | Red |
| 87 | Flashfires | Red |
| 88 | Flight | Blue |
| 89 | Fog | Green |
| 90* | Force of Nature | Green |
| 91 | Forcefield | Artifact |
| 92 | Forest | None |
| 93 | Forest | None |
| 94* | Forest | None |
| 95 | Fork | Red |
| 96 | Frozen Shade | Black |
| 97 | Fungusaur | Green |
| 98 | Gaea's Liege | Green |
| 99 | Gauntlet of Might | Artifact |
| 100 | Giant Growth | Green |
| 101 | Giant Spider | Green |
| 102 | Glasses of Urza | Artifact |
| 103 | Gloom | Black |
| 104 | Goblin Balloon Brigade | Red |
| 105 | Goblin King | Red |
| 106 | Granite Gargoyle | Red |
| 107 | Gray Ogre | Red |
| 108 | Green Ward | White |
| 109 | Grizzly Bears | Green |
| 110 | Guardian Angel | White |
| 111 | Healing Salve | White |
| 112 | Helm of Chatzuk | Artifact |

| TYPE | ARTIST'S NAME | COMMONALITY |
|------|---------------|-------------|
| Enchantment | Quinton Hoover | Common |
| Sorcery | Dan Frazier | Rare |
| Creature | Anson Maddocks | Rare |
| Enchantment | Sandra Everingham | Uncommon |
| Instant | Anson Maddocks | Common |
| Enchantment | Mark Poole | Rare |
| Enchantment | Mark Poole | Rare |
| Enchantment | Mark Poole | Common |
| Enchantment | Quinton Hoover | Uncommon |
| Creature | Melissa Benson | Uncommon |
| Sorcery | Mark Tedin | Common |
| Enchantment | Dan Frazier | Common |
| Sorcery | Dameon Willich | Uncommon |
| Enchantment | Anson Maddocks | Common |
| Instant | Jesper Myrfors | Common |
| Creature | Douglas Shuler | Rare |
| Poly | Dan Frazier | Rare |
| Land | Christopher Rush | Most Common |
| Land | Christopher Rush | Most Common |
| Land | Christopher Rush | Most Common |
| Interrupt | Amy Weber | Rare |
| Creature | Douglas Shuler | Common |
| Creature | Daniel Gelon | Rare |
| Creature | Dameon Willich | Rare |
| Continuous | Christopher Rush | Rare |
| Instant | Sandra Everingham | Common |
| Creature | Sandra Everingham | Common |
| Mono | Douglas Shuler | Uncommon |
| Enchantment | Dan Frazier | Uncommon |
| Creature | Andi Rusu | Uncommon |
| Creature | Jesper Myrfors | Rare |
| Creature | Christopher Rush | Rare |
| Creature | Dan Frazier | Common |
| Enchantment | Dan Frazier | Uncommon |
| Creature | Jeff A. Menges | Common |
| Instant | Anson Maddocks | Common |
| Instant | Dan Frazier | Common |
| Mono | Mark Tedin | Rare |

| | CARD NAME | COLOR |
|------|-----------|-------|
| 113 | Hill Giant | Red |
| 114 | The Hive | Artifact |
| 115 | Holy Armor | White |
| 116 | Holy Strength | White |
| 117 | Howl from Beyond | Black |
| 118 | Howling Mine | Artifact |
| 119 | Hurloon Minotaur | Red |
| 120 | Hurricane | Green |
| 121 | Hypnotic Specter | Black |
| 122 | Ice Storm | Green |
| 123* | Icy Manipulator | Artifact |
| 124 | Illusionary Mask | Artifact |
| 125 | Instill Energy | Green |
| 126 | Invisibility | Blue |
| 127 | Iron Star | Artifact |
| 128 | Ironclaw Orcs | Red |
| 129 | Ironroot Treefolk | Green |
| 130 | Island | None |
| 131 | Island | None |
| 132* | Island | None |
| 133* | Island Sanctuary | White |
| 134 | Ivory Cup | Artifact |
| 135 | Jade Monolith | Artifact |
| 136 | Jade Statue | Artifact |
| 137 | Jayemdae Tome | Artifact |
| 138 | Juggernaut | Artifact |
| 139 | Jump | Blue |
| 140* | Karma | White |
| 141 | Keldon Warlord | Red |
| 142 | Kormus Bell | Artifact |
| 143 | Kudzu | Green |
| 144 | Lance | White |
| 145 | Ley Druid | Green |
| 146 | Library of Leng | Artifact |
| 147 | Lich | Black |
| 148 | Lifeforce | Green |
| 149 | Lifelace | Green |
| 150 | Lifetap | Blue |

| TYPE | ARTIST'S NAME | COMMONALITY |
|------|---------------|-------------|
| Creature | Dan Frazier | Common |
| Mono | Sandra Everingham | Rare |
| Enchantment | Melissa Benson | Common |
| Enchantment | Anson Maddocks | Common |
| Instant | Mark Poole | Common |
| Continuous | Mark Poole | Rare |
| Creature | Anson Maddocks | Common |
| Sorcery | Dameon Willich | Uncommon |
| Creature | Douglas Shuler | Uncommon |
| Sorcery | Dan Frazier | Uncommon |
| Mono | Douglas Shuler | Uncommon |
| Poly | Amy Weber | Rare |
| Enchantment | Dameon Willich | Uncommon |
| Enchantment | Anson Maddocks | Common |
| Poly | Dan Frazier | Uncommon |
| Creature | Anson Maddocks | Common |
| Creature | Jesper Myrfors | Common |
| Land | Mark Poole | Most Common |
| Land | Mark Poole | Most Common |
| Land | Mark Poole | Most Common |
| Enchantment | Mark Poole | Rare |
| Poly | Anson Maddocks | Uncommon |
| Poly | Anson Maddocks | Rare |
| Artifact | Dan Frazier | Uncommon |
| Mono | Mark Tedin | Rare |
| Creature | Dan Frazier | Uncommon |
| Instant | Mark Poole | Common |
| Enchantment | Richard Thomas | Uncommon |
| Creature | Kev Brockschmidt | Uncommon |
| Continuous | Christopher Rush | Rare |
| Enchantment | Mark Poole | Rare |
| Enchantment | Rob Alexander | Uncommon |
| Creature | Sandra Everingham | Uncommon |
| Continuous | Daniel Gelon | Uncommon |
| Enchantment | Daniel Gelon | Rare |
| Enchantment | Dameon Willich | Uncommon |
| Interrupt | Amy Weber | Rare |
| Enchantment | Anson Maddocks | Uncommon |

| | CARD NAME | COLOR |
|---|---|---|
| 151 | Lightning Bolt | Red |
| 152 | Living Artifact | Green |
| 153 | Living Lands | Green |
| 154 | Living Wall | Artifact |
| 155 | Llanowar Elves | Green |
| 156 | Lord of Atlantis | Blue |
| 157 | Lord of the Pit | Black |
| 158 | Lure | Green |
| 159 | Magical Hack | Blue |
| 160 | Mahamoti Djinn | Blue |
| 161 | Mana Flare | Red |
| 162* | Mana Short | Blue |
| 163 | Mana Vault | Artifact |
| 164 | Manabarbs | Red |
| 165 | Meekstone | Artifact |
| 166 | Merfolk of the Pearl Trident | Blue |
| 167 | Mesa Pegasus | White |
| 168 | Mind Twist | Black |
| 169 | Mons's Goblin Raiders | Red |
| 170 | Mountain | None |
| 171 | Mountain | None |
| 172* | Mountain | None |
| 173 | Mox Emerald | Artifact |
| 174 | Mox Jet | Artifact |
| 175 | Mox Pearl | Artifact |
| 176 | Mox Ruby | Artifact |
| 177 | Mox Sapphire | Artifact |
| 178 | Natural Selection | Green |
| 179 | Nether Shadow | Black |
| 180 | Nettling Imp | Black |
| 181 | Nevinyrral's Disk | Artifact |
| 182* | Nightmare | Black |
| 183 | Northern Paladin | White |
| 184 | Obsianus Golem | Artifact |
| 185* | Orcish Artillery | Red |
| 186* | Orcish Oriflamme | Red |
| 187 | Paralyze | Black |
| 188 | Pearled Unicorn | White |

| TYPE | ARTIST'S NAME | COMMONALITY |
|------|---------------|-------------|
| Instant | Christopher Rush | Common |
| Enchantment | Anson Maddocks | Rare |
| Enchantment | Jesper Myrfors | Rare |
| Creature | Anson Maddocks | Uncommon |
| Creature | Anson Maddocks | Common |
| Creature | Melissa Benson | Rare |
| Creature | Mark Tedin | Rare |
| Enchantment | Anson Maddocks | Uncommon |
| Interrupt | Julie Baroh | Rare |
| Creature | Dan Frazier | Rare |
| Enchantment | Christopher Rush | Rare |
| Instant | Dameon Willich | Rare |
| Mono | Mark Tedin | Rare |
| Enchantment | Christopher Rush | Rare |
| Continuous | Quinton Hoover | Rare |
| Creature | Jeff A. Menges | Common |
| Creature | Melissa Benson | Common |
| Sorcery | Julie Baroh | Rare |
| Creature | Jeff A. Menges | Common |
| Land | Douglas Shuler | Most Common |
| Land | Douglas Shuler | Most Common |
| Land | Douglas Shuler | Most Common |
| Mono | Dan Frazier | Rare |
| Mono | Dan Frazier | Rare |
| Mono | Dan Frazier | Rare |
| Mono | Dan Frazier | Rare |
| Mono | Dan Frazier | Rare |
| Instant | Mark Poole | Rare |
| Creature | Christopher Rush | Rare |
| Creature | Quinton Hoover | Uncommon |
| Mono | Mark Tedin | Rare |
| Creature | Melissa Benson | Rare |
| Creature | Douglas Shuler | Rare |
| Creature | Jesper Myrfors | Uncommon |
| Creature | Anson Maddocks | Uncommon |
| Enchantment | Dan Frazier | Uncommon |
| Enchantment | Anson Maddocks | Common |
| Creature | Cornelius Brudi | Common |

| | CARD NAME | COLOR |
|---|---|---|
| 189 | Personal Incarnation | White |
| 190 | Pestilence | Black |
| 191* | Phantasmal Forces | Blue |
| 192 | Phantasmal Terrain | Blue |
| 193 | Phantom Monster | Blue |
| 194 | Pirate Ship | Blue |
| 195 | Plague Rats | Black |
| 196 | Plains | None |
| 197 | Plains | None |
| 198* | Plains | None |
| 199 | Plateau | None |
| 200 | Power Leak | Blue |
| 201 | Power Sink | Blue |
| 202 | Power Surge | Red |
| 203 | Prodigal Sorcerer | Blue |
| 204 | Psionic Blast | Blue |
| 205 | Psychic Venom | Blue |
| 206 | Purelace | White |
| 207 | Raging River | Red |
| 208 | Raise Dead | Black |
| 209* | Red Elemental Blast | Red |
| 210 | Red Ward | White |
| 211 | Regeneration | Green |
| 212 | Regrowth | Green |
| 213 | Resurrection | White |
| 214 | Reverse Damage | White |
| 215 | Righteousness | White |
| 216 | Roc of Kher Ridges | Red |
| 217* | Rock Hydra | Red |
| 218 | Rod of Ruin | Artifact |
| 219 | Royal Assassin | Black |
| 220 | Sacrifice | Black |
| 221 | Samite Healer | White |
| 222 | Savannah | None |
| 223 | Savannah Lions | White |
| 224 | Scathe Zombies | Black |
| 225 | Scavenging Ghoul | Black |
| 226 | Scrubland | None |

| TYPE | ARTIST'S NAME | COMMONALITY |
|------|---------------|-------------|
| Creature | Kev Brockschmidt | Rare |
| Enchantment | Jesper Myrfors | Common |
| Creature | Mark Poole | Uncommon |
| Enchantment | Dameon Willich | Common |
| Creature | Jesper Myrfors | Uncommon |
| Creature | Tom Wänerstrand | Rare |
| Creature | Anson Maddocks | Common |
| Land | Jesper Myrfors | Most Common |
| Land | Jesper Myrfors | Most Common |
| Land | Jesper Myrfors | Most Common |
| Land | Drew Tucker | Rare |
| Enchantment | Drew Tucker | Common |
| Interrupt | Richard Thomas | Common |
| Enchantment | Douglas Shuler | Rare |
| Creature | Douglas Shuler | Common |
| Instant | Douglas Shuler | Uncommon |
| Enchantment | Brian Snoddy | Common |
| Interrupt | Sandra Everingham | Rare |
| Enchantment | Sandra Everingham | Rare |
| Sorcery | Jeff A. Menges | Common |
| Interrupt | Richard Thomas | Common |
| Enchantment | Dan Frazier | Uncommon |
| Enchantment | Quinton Hoover | Common |
| Sorcery | Dameon Willich | Uncommon |
| Sorcery | Dan Frazier | Uncommon |
| Instant | Dameon Willich | Rare |
| Instant | Douglas Shuler | Rare |
| Creature | Andi Rusu | Rare |
| Creature | Jeff A. Menges | Rare |
| Mono | Christopher Rush | Uncommon |
| Creature | Tom Wänerstrand | Rare |
| Interrupt | Dan Frazier | Uncommon |
| Creature | Tom Wänerstrand | Common |
| Land | Rob Alexander | Rare |
| Creature | Daniel Gelon | Rare |
| Creature | Jesper Myrfors | Common |
| Creature | Jeff A. Menges | Uncommon |
| Land | Jesper Myrfors | Rare |

| | CARD NAME | COLOR |
|---|---|---|
| 227 | Scryb Sprites | Green |
| 228 | Sea Serpent | Blue |
| 229* | Sedge Troll | Red |
| 230 | Sengir Vampire | Black |
| 231 | Serra Angel | White |
| 232 | Shanodin Dryads | Green |
| 233 | Shatter | Red |
| 234 | Shivan Dragon | Red |
| 235 | Simulacrum | Black |
| 236 | Sinkhole | Black |
| 237 | Siren's Call | Blue |
| 238 | Sleight of Mind | Blue |
| 239 | Smoke | Red |
| 240 | Sol Ring | Artifact |
| 241 | Soul Net | Artifact |
| 242 | Spell Blast | Blue |
| 243 | Stasis | Blue |
| 244 | Steal Artifact | Blue |
| 245 | Stone Giant | Red |
| 246 | Stone Rain | Red |
| 247 | Stream of Life | Green |
| 248 | Sunglasses of Urza | Artifact |
| 249 | Swamp | None |
| 250 | Swamp | None |
| 251* | Swamp | None |
| 252 | Swords to Plowshares | White |
| 253 | Taiga | None |
| 254 | Terror | Black |
| 255 | Thicket Basilisk | Green |
| 256 | Thoughtlace | Blue |
| 257 | Throne of Bone | Artifact |
| 258 | Timber Wolves | Green |
| 259 | Time Vault | Artifact |
| 260 | Time Walk | Blue |
| 261 | Timetwister | Blue |
| 262 | Tranquility | Green |
| 263* | Tropical Island | None |
| 264 | Tsunami | Green |

| TYPE | ARTIST'S NAME | COMMONALITY |
| --- | --- | --- |
| Creature | Amy Weber | Common |
| Creature | Jeff A. Menges | Common |
| Creature | Dan Frazier | Rare |
| Creature | Anson Maddocks | Uncommon |
| Creature | Douglas Shuler | Uncommon |
| Creature | Anson Maddocks | Common |
| Instant | Amy Weber | Common |
| Creature | Melissa Benson | Rare |
| Instant | Mark Poole | Uncommon |
| Sorcery | Sandra Everingham | Common |
| Instant | Anson Maddocks | Uncommon |
| Interrupt | Mark Poole | Rare |
| Enchantment | Jesper Myrfors | Rare |
| Mono | Mark Tedin | Uncommon |
| Poly | Dameon Willich | Uncommon |
| Interrupt | Brian Snoddy | Common |
| Enchantment | Fay Jones | Rare |
| Enchantment | Amy Weber | Uncommon |
| Creature | Dameon Willich | Uncommon |
| Sorcery | Daniel Gelon | Common |
| Sorcery | Mark Poole | Common |
| Continuous | Dan Frazier | Rare |
| Land | Dan Frazier | Most Common |
| Land | Dan Frazier | Most Common |
| Land | Dan Frazier | Most Common |
| Instant | Jeff A. Menges | Uncommon |
| Land | Rob Alexander | Rare |
| Instant | Ron Spencer | Common |
| Creature | Dan Frazier | Uncommon |
| Interrupt | Mark Poole | Rare |
| Poly | Anson Maddocks | Uncommon |
| Creature | Melissa Benson | Rare |
| Mono | Mark Tedin | Rare |
| Sorcery | Amy Weber | Rare |
| Sorcery | Mark Tedin | Rare |
| Sorcery | Douglas Shuler | Common |
| Land | Jesper Myrfors | Rare |
| Sorcery | Richard Thomas | Uncommon |

| | CARD NAME | COLOR |
|---|---|---|
| 265 | Tundra | None |
| 266 | Tunnel | Red |
| 267* | Twiddle | Blue |
| 268 | Two-Headed Giant | Red |
| 269 | Underground Sea | None |
| 270 | Unholy Strength | Black |
| 271* | Unsummon | Blue |
| 272 | Uthden Troll | Red |
| 273 | Verduran Enchantress | Green |
| 274 | Vesuvan Doppelganger | Blue |
| 275 | Veteran Bodyguard | White |
| 276 | Volcanic Eruption | Blue |
| 277* | Volcanic Island | None |
| 278 | Wall of Air | Blue |
| 279 | Wall of Bone | Black |
| 280 | Wall of Brambles | Green |
| 281 | Wall of Fire | Red |
| 282 | Wall of Ice | Green |
| 283 | Wall of Stone | Red |
| 284 | Wall of Swords | White |
| 285 | Wall of Water | Blue |
| 286 | Wall of Wood | Green |
| 287 | Wanderlust | Green |
| 288 | War Mammoth | Green |
| 289 | Warp Artifact | Black |
| 290 | Water Elemental | Blue |
| 291 | Weakness | Black |
| 292 | Web | Green |
| 293 | Wheel of Fortune | Red |
| 294 | White Knight | White |
| 295 | White Ward | White |
| 296 | Wild Growth | Green |
| 297 | Will-O'-The-Wisp | Black |
| 298 | Winter Orb | Artifact |
| 299 | Wooden Sphere | Artifact |
| 300 | Word of Command | Black |
| 301 | Wrath of God | White |
| 302 | Zombie Master | Black |

| TYPE | ARTIST'S NAME | COMMONALITY |
|------|---------------|-------------|
| Land | Jesper Myrfors | Rare |
| Instant | Dan Frazier | Uncommon |
| Instant | Rob Alexander | Common |
| Creature | Anson Maddocks | Rare |
| Land | Rob Alexander | Rare |
| Enchantment | Douglas Shuler | Common |
| Instant | Douglas Shuler | Common |
| Creature | Douglas Shuler | Uncommon |
| Creature | Kev Brockschmidt | Rare |
| Creature | Quinton Hoover | Rare |
| Creature | Douglas Shuler | Rare |
| Sorcery | Douglas Shuler | Rare |
| Land | Brian Snoddy | Rare |
| Creature | Richard Thomas | Uncommon |
| Creature | Anson Maddocks | Uncommon |
| Creature | Anson Maddocks | Uncommon |
| Creature | Richard Thomas | Uncommon |
| Creature | Richard Thomas | Uncommon |
| Creature | Dan Frazier | Uncommon |
| Creature | Mark Tedin | Uncommon |
| Creature | Richard Thomas | Uncommon |
| Creature | Mark Tedin | Common |
| Enchantment | Cornelius Brudi | Uncommon |
| Creature | Jeff A. Menges | Common |
| Enchantment | Amy Weber | Rare |
| Creature | Jeff A. Menges | Uncommon |
| Enchantment | Douglas Shuler | Common |
| Enchantment | Rob Alexander | Rare |
| Sorcery | Daniel Gelon | Rare |
| Creature | Daniel Gelon | Uncommon |
| Enchantment | Dan Frazier | Uncommon |
| Enchantment | Mark Poole | Common |
| Creature | Jesper Myrfors | Rare |
| Continuous | Mark Tedin | Rare |
| Poly | Mark Tedin | Uncommon |
| Instant | Jesper Myrfors | Rare |
| Sorcery | Quinton Hoover | Rare |
| Creature | Jeff A. Menges | Rare |

# Collector's Notes

12 **Basalt Monolith:** The Alpha version had no mana symbol in the text.

16 **Birds Of Paradise:** The Alpha version had two slashes in text.

31 **Channel:** The Alpha version had the phrase "Effects that prevent damage..."

34 **Circle Of Protection: Black**: This card was inadvertently left out of the Alpha version.

37 **Circle Of Protection: Red:** The Alpha version miscredited Anson Maddocks as the artist.

55 **Cyclopean Tomb:** The Alpha version was missing the casting cost.

58 **Death Ward:** The Alpha version miscredited Dan Frazier as the artist.

62 **Demonic Hordes:** The Alpha version had "BBB" in place of black mana symbols.

69 **Drain Life:** The Alpha version had a "B" in place of the black mana symbol.

77 **Elvish Archers:** The Alpha version listed the power and toughness as 1/2 instead of 2/1.

90 **Force Of Nature:** The Alpha print version had "GGGG" in place of green mana symbols.

94 **Forest:** The third forest was not included in the Alpha print run.

123 **Icy Manipulator:** The Alpha version did not include the phrase "No effects are generated by the target card." Additionally, the spelling "Schuler" was corrected in Beta and subsequent versions.

132 **Island:** The third Island was not included in the Alpha version.

133 **Island Sanctuary:** The Alpha version had the word "damage" instead of "attack."

140 **Karma:** The Alpha version had the words "during his or her upkeep."

162 **Mana Short:** The Alpha version did not include the phrase "Opponent takes no damage...."

172 **Mountain:** The third Mountain was not included in the Alpha version.

182 **Nightmare:** The Beta print run had lettering flaws in the word "swamp."

185 **Orcish Artillery:** The Alpha version casting cost was one indefinite and one red mana.

186 **Orcish Oriflamme:** The Alpha version casting cost was one indefinite and one red mana.

191 **Phantasmal Forces:** The Alpha version had a "U" in place of the blue mana symbol.

198 **Plains:** The third Plains was not included in the Alpha version.

209 **Red Elemental Blast:** The Alpha version listed the spell type as "Instant."

217 **Rock Hydra:** The Alpha print version had "R" in place of the red mana symbol.

229 **Sedge Troll:** The Alpha version miscredited Jeff A. Menges as the artist.

251 **Swamp:** The third Swamp was not in the Alpha version.

263 **Tropical Island:** The Alpha version miscredited Mark Poole as the artist.

267 **Twiddle:** The Alpha version did not have the phrase "No effects are generated by the target card."

271 **Unsummon:** The Alpha version had the word "CARD ed instead of "discarded."

277 **Volcanic Island:** This card was inadvertently left out of the Alpha version.

In the first print run, every instance of Douglas Shuler's name was mispelled "Schuler". This misspelling appears on the following cards: Animate Artifact, Benalish Hero, Circle of Protection: White, Contract From Below, Demonic Tutor, Drain Life, Drain Power, Dwarven Warriors, Force of Nature, Frozen Shade, Glasses of Urza, Hypnotic Specter, Icy Manipulator, Mountain, Northern Paladin, Power Surge, Prodigal Sorcerer, Righteousness, Serra Angel, Tranquility, Unholy Strength, Unsummon, Uthden Troll, Veteran Bodyguard, Weakness.

# A Note On Expansion Sets

From time to time, the world of **Magic** grows with the release of an "expansion set." These are additional card sets, generally between fifty and four hundred cards, that players may incorporate into their existing decks. Expansion sets generally follow themes: the first expansion set for *Magic: The Gathering*, for example, was inspired by the tales and characters of *A Thousand And One Arabian Nights*. Each new expansion alters the overall flavor of the game, changing the card balance and forcing players to redefine their current game strategies.

This regular infusion of new cards will constantly change the dynamics of the duel and pose new challenges to trading and deck-building. As the players' familiarity with the world of **Magic** grows, so does the card pool, ensuring that there will always be unknown and surprising elements in the game. Expansion sets are also an opportunity to develop the character of Dominia, the multiverse within which *Magic: The Gathering* is set. Dominia is immense; expansion sets allow game designers and players to explore new parts of it, and discover aspects of the "old" world that new cards can uncover.

To preserve the collecting value of the cards, each expansion will be a limited release. Some of the cards may then be incorporated into later editions of *Magic: The Gathering* decks, so that the environment in that game is always being refreshed. No new card will be added to the *Magic: The Gathering* series without first appearing in an expansion; this way, players and collectors are not forced to purchase a whole set of *Magic: The Gathering* cards to obtain a few new additions.

# VII

# Supplementary Material & Game Support

## •The Duelists' Convocation and Other Player Resources

For the **Magic** enthusiast, the official **Deckmaster** players' organization has a lot to offer

## •*Magic: The Gathering* Frequently Asked Questions (FAQ)

Months of feedback from players has produced a long list of answers to the game's most common confusions.

## •Glossary

## •Index

## •Duelists' Convocation Application

## •Magic: The Gathering Customer Survey

# The Duelists' Convocation and Other Player Resources

## The Duelists' Convocation

The Duelists' Convocation is the players organization that Wizards of the Coast developed for enthusiasts of *Magic: The Gathering* and the other **Deckmaster** games that will be released. Through the Convocation, players can participate in weekly league activities at their local game shops (or other suitable locations) with other members. These activities offer valuable trading opportunities and allow players to refine their dueling and deck building skills in preparation for **Magic** tournaments already being held at many of the game conventions around the world. At these tournaments, players from that area compete for prizes and national ranking points, which then contribute to a national standing.

### *The Duelist*

Two publications were developed to support the Convocation's activities. *The Duelist* is a quarterly full-color magazine established to promote the growing genre of collectable trading card games. Every issue features reviews of the latest trading card products, articles on game variants, previews of upcoming **Deckmaster** releases, interviews with artists and designers, news from the tournament circuit, and tips on play. The collectors' information and classified sections of the magazine offer Duelists' Convocation members a reliable way of communicating with each other. In the months that *The Duelist* is not published, a more informal newsletter called the *Duelists' Companion* keeps members up to date on Convocation news and events.

## Other Product Services

We encourage you to write to us if you have any questions or concerns about *Magic: The Gathering*. Write to:

> Wizards of the Coast
> P.O. Box 707
> Renton WA 98057–0707
> ATTN: **Magic** Questions

## More Help

We also provide electronic support. We have an e-mail list, company representatives on the Internet and many commercial services, and more. For information on these services, send e-mail to questions@wizards.com and we'll get right back to you. (Refer to the end of the FAQ contained in this book for more information on product support for electronic media.)

## Acquiring Original Artwork

If you'd like to acquire the original artwork for one of these cards, write us. If we know the piece you want is available for sale, we'll tell you how to reach the owner.

## *Magic: The Gathering* Frequently Asked Questions (FAQ)

*Compiled by Dave Howell, Beth Moursund, and James Ernest*

This list of questions is intended to clarify the First Edition *Magic: The Gathering* rules. It applies to the Revised Edition as well. These questions and answers are not meant to supercede or be a substitute for the rules. If any answer below actually modifies or corrects the old published rules, it will make that clear. This list is based on the *Shahrazad Tells All* Edition, accurate as of the date of publication. To obtain the latest copy, see the information at the end of this FAQ.

### SEQUENCE OF PLAY

**Q:** What exactly *is* the turn order?

**A:** Every turn consists of six phases: Untap, Upkeep, Draw, Main, Discard, and End. All but one of these phases is usually very fast. They all exist to support the Main Phase. In particular, the following describes what can happen in each Phase. (Note that there may be cards which break these rules. If they do, the *card* will tell you how. These detailed phase descriptions also contain certain restrictions which do not appear in the rules; they exist only to deal with a small number of paradoxical events.)

1. **UNTAP:** All of your cards in play can and must untap, and all do so simultaneously. You may not cast spells or use any other effects either before or during Untap.

2. **UPKEEP:** Any cards which require upkeep will tell you; otherwise, you don't have to do anything in this phase. Fast effects may be used by either player during Upkeep, including those which prevent damage you may have suffered during Untap.

3. **DRAW:** You can and must draw one card from your Library. If you must draw and are out of cards, you lose the game. Fast effects may be used by either player during Draw.

4. **MAIN:** During the main phase, you may do the following, in any order:

   a. play one land card;
   b. make one attack (see **Attack**, below); or
   c. cast spells (see **Spells**, below).

   You may only lay out one land, and you may only make one Attack.

   However, there is no limit to the number of spells you may cast, as long as you can afford their casting cost, and you may cast spells at any time during the Main Phase.

5. **DISCARD:** If you have more then seven cards in your hand, you must discard until you have only seven. If you have seven or less, you may not discard, even if you want to. Fast effects may be used by either player during Discard.

6. **END:** It's rarely obvious that your turn is over; therefore, you must tell your opponent that you're done. When you announce that

your turn is over, you're really saying that this is your opponent's last chance to cast fast effects on your turn. You may respond with fast effects of your own as well.

7. **HEAL CREATURES:** Now the turn is over. All damage is cleared from creatures, and all fast effects expire. You may not cast spells or use any other effects during or after this phase. One exception: if a creature is going to die, you may use damage prevention and regeneration as usual.

**Q:** What's the order of an Attack Phase?

**A:** You only get one each turn, and your mana pool clears at the beginning and end of it. During the attack, only fast effects may be used; no sorceries may be cast, and no lands, creatures, or artifacts can come into play. It goes like this:

1. Announce attack; last chance for either player to use pre-attack fast effects.
2. Declare and tap attacking creatures.
3. Either player may use fast effects.
4. Declare blocking.
5. Either player may use fast effects. Note that if a blocking creature is removed or a blocked attacking creature rendered unblockable during this step, the attacking creature is still blocked.
6. Assign damage.
7. Either player may use damage-prevention, damage-redirection, regeneration, and life-giving fast effects. The only other fast effects that may be used at this time are interrupts.

8.  Creatures which have lethal damage go to the graveyard.
9.  Any effects triggered by the deaths (**Vampires** gaining counters, **Creature Bond** damage, the use of **Soul Net**, and so on) take place. Only fast effects triggered by the deaths may be used.

Note that steps 2, 4, 6, and 8 are considered instantaneous, and you may not use any fast effects during them.

Steps 6–9 happen twice if the combat includes any creatures with the First Strike ability. Steps 6–9 also happen any time that any spell or fast effect causes damage.

**Q:** When exactly can I cast Spells? And what the heck are fast effects?

**A:** Fast effects include instants, interrupts, and most special powers of cards in play, including the tapping of land for mana. Fast effects are called that because a Fast Effect can start before another spell has finished. Tapping mana is played with the speed of an interrupt. All other special powers are assumed to occur with the speed of an instant. These include tapping the **Prodigal Sorcerer** to poke somebody; using a **Pestilence** to poke everybody; putting more power into an existing **Holy Armor** (to keep your **Sorcerer** from dying from the **Pestilence**, for example); and so forth.

You can use fast effects during either player's Upkeep, Draw, Main, Discard, and End phases, and during specific parts of an Attack. They may not be played during Untap or Heal Creatures, or during damage resolution except as indicated above. This sounds like an extreme change from the rules, which say "you may use fast effects at any time," but these other phases are defined as instantaneous, and in all but a very few cases, there's no difference between using a fast effect during an instantaneous phase, and using it during an adjoining legal period.

Any spell that isn't an instant or an interrupt can only be played during the Main Phase of your turn. Remember that they're only spells as long as they're in your hand. Once in play, cards represent creatures, artifacts, enchantments, or whatever. So, for example, you may only cast **Holy Armor** (an enchantment) onto your Sorcerer during your main phase, but you may then power it up whenever you like. Note also that lands are never considered spells, even in your hand. Laying out a land can't be counterspelled.

**Q:** If a spell requires a target, can I cast it without one?

**A:** No. Targeting is poorly defined in the old rulebooks. If you can choose the victim of a spell (for example, "enchant flying creature",) then the spell needs a target. If a spell says something like "destroys all plains in play," however, then it may be cast with no applicable target.

**Q:** What happens if the target of an enchantment becomes ineligible after the enchantment has been cast? For example, **Earthbind** enchants a flying creature by removing its flying ability.

**A:** In the old rules, the enchantment remains even if the target becomes illegal (for example, if you play an "enchant non-creature artifact" card on an artifact which becomes a creature, or an "enchant land" card on a land that becomes a creature). In the Revised Edition rules, this has changed: invalid enchantments are removed.

**Q:** Please translate this: "(B): Bounces."

**A:** In the case of enchantments and creature powers, it reads: "For each B spent, this card will bounce." (That is, regenerate, jump, gain +1/+1, whatever.) If this taps the creature, the text will make this clear. Otherwise they may be used as many times per turn as you wish, and they are fast effects. However, in the case of artifacts, the translation is just a little different. If it is a mono artifact (First Edition cards), using it will tap it. If it is a poly artifact (also First Edition cards), it can still only be used once per event. For example, take Ivory Cup: "(1): Any white spell cast by any player gives you 1 life." If you translated this like a creature fast effect, then you could spend five mana points in response to *one* white spell and get five life points. Instead, you can use these kinds of artifacts several times, but only in response to several events.

**Q:** What is the mana pool and when does it clear?

**A:** Technically, when you cast a spell, you first tap the mana points from whatever source you wish (land, usually). These points go into your mana pool. Then, as a separate event, you spend those points on the casting of a spell. At the end of every phase, and at the beginning and end of an attack, your mana pool clears. If you had any points left over, you take a point of damage from each one as it leaves. And no, you can't use a **Circle of Protection** against this—unspent mana are considered a colorless source of damage.

## TIMING

**Q:** What's the difference between an **instant** and an **interrupt**?

**A:** Interrupts happen the moment they are cast, and instants all line up before any of them take effect. Instants can't cancel each other. In other words, once your opponent performs any fast effect which is defined to happen with the speed of an instant, you can't stop it from happening with another instant. Once everybody is through casting their instants, they all happen simultaneously. If I cast **Lightning Bolt** (an Instant) on your **Scryb Sprites** (1/1), they will take 3 points of damage. If you respond by casting **Giant Growth** on them (an Instant, which conveys +3/+3), they will still take 3 points of damage, survive, and be equivalent to a 4/4 creature with 3 points of damage till the end of the turn.

Interrupts, however, can stop spells and other events from happening altogether. If, instead of using a **Giant Growth**, you cast a **Blue Elemental Blast** (an interrupt) on my **Lightning Bolt**, it would stop my **Lighting Bolt** from ever happening, and the **Sprites** would stay blissfully ignorant of the whole affair.

Now, I still have the option of interrupting your

interrupt, say, with a **Red Elemental Blast,** which would let my **Lightning Bolt** sneak through...

A note on counterspells: countered spells go to the graveyard, and the mana points are considered spent. The card does not go back into your hand, nor does the mana remain in your pool.

Also note that destroying the card that is the source of an effect does not counter the effect, even if the destruction is an interrupt. If you tap a **Prodigal Sorcerer** to do a point of damage to me and I respond by destroying the **Sorcerer** with a **Red Elemental Blast,** the damage still happens.

**Q:** Which fast effects are interrupts?

**A:** In general, tapping a source of mana is considered to happen with the speed of an interrupt. (Otherwise, you wouldn't ever be able to cast an interrupt spell.) Other creature effects, enchantments, artifacts, and so on, work with the speed of instants unless they say otherwise.

**Q:** Timing: Let's say I cast a spell that does 5 points of damage to every creature and both players. My opponent has 4 points of life, 3 small creatures, some available mana, and a Soul Net. The **Soul Net** is an artifact which will give him a life point every time a creature dies (he pays 1 mana for each creature). Is he dead, or not?

**A:** No. Only check for player death at the end of a phase, and the beginning or end of an attack. The 3 creatures die and he loses 5 life points. Then immediately after that he taps 3 mana and uses the **Soul Net** to gain 3 life points. Result: he's creatureless, tapped, and has 2 life points left. Of course, you can't use the Soul Net on a creature that doesn't actually go to the graveyard, for example, one that is regenerated.

**Q:** Okay, now let's say we are both close to death: he has 2 life points and I have 3. I cast **Lightning Bolt.** He responds by returning a Lightning Bolt. Who wins?

**A:** Nobody. The spells are instants, and are assumed to happen at the same time, unless one of you can interrupt one of them.

**Q:** But he's got fewer life points than me. Doesn't that count for anything?

**A:** No. Dead is still dead. This game is a draw.

## WARDS and PROTECTION

**Q:** I have a **Circle of Protection: Red** ("(1): Prevents all damage against you from one red source..."). Can I use this more than once per turn?

**A:** Yes. Spend one point of mana for each source you wish to squelch. If a single source somehow manages to damage you twice, pay another mana as if it were another source.

**Q:** Can a **Circle of Protection** protect my creatures?

**A:** No. It only prevents you from being damaged. A **Lightning Bolt** can still kill your Orcs, and a **Stone Rain** can still destroy your land.

**Q:** What color are artifacts? The artifacts look brown to me. And what color are lands?

**A:** Lands and artifacts are defined as colorless. There isn't a Circle of Protection: Colorless. Damage from unspent mana is also considered to come from a colorless source, so you can't use a Circle of Protection: Red to keep from taking damage from unspent red mana points.

**Q:** I'm taking damage from a Green creature (**Llanowar Elves**) with a Red enchantment (**Firebreathing,** which gives +1/+0). What color is the source of the damage?

**A:** In this case, Green. A **Circle of Protection: Red** won't help you.

**Q:** I'm taking damage from tapping a land (colorless) because there's a **Psychic Venom** on it (Blue). Now what?

**A:** In this case, the enchantment is considered to be dealing the damage. The difference is this: in the case of **Firebreathing,** the creature's own power is being increased by the enchantment. In the case of a **Psychic Venom,** the damage comes directly from the enchantment, since land doesn't normally damage you at all. Note also that by this ruling, damage from a **Wanderlust** is considered Green.

**Q:** In the case of creatures and wards, what's "protection from blue"? Exactly how is it defined?

**A:** Not very well. We're sorry about not being clear on

the finer points of Protection from a color. The rules in the First Edition were as follows:

> A creature with protection from blue cannot be affected by any blue magic. In specific, it:
>
> • cannot be blocked by blue creatures
> • cannot be damaged by blue creatures
> • cannot be enchanted, damaged, or otherwise affected by Blue cards
>
> Damage done by this creature *cannot* be prevented by blue cards.

This caused a lot of problems. In the current rules, a creature with protection from Blue:

• cannot be damaged by blue spells or creatures
• cannot be blocked by blue creatures
• cannot be the target of further blue spells, and any enchantments of that color already on the creature are dispelled.

However, cards of a given color can be used to prevent damage done by a creature with protection from that color. For example, damage done by this creature *can* be prevented by blue cards. A **Circle of Protection** will stop damage done by a white warded creature. (Are you confused yet?)

We apologize that the First Edition rules on protection are unclear and riddled with paradoxes. For this reason, we suggest that you use the Revised Edition rules.

## CREATURE ABILITIES

**Q:** Regeneration: Can I regenerate a creature that died last turn?

**A:** No. Regeneration only prevents a creature from going to the graveyard. If you can't manage it right away, it won't work at all.

**Q:** Can I attack or defend with a creature that's tapped?

**A:** No.

**Q:** Can I attack with a creature I've just summoned?

**A:** No. Nor can you do anything else that requires tapping it until your next turn. The creature is suffering from what we call "summoning sickness." Basically, it just got here, and your opponent has a turn to react before the creature starts working. You are allowed to defend with the creature on your opponent's next turn, because defending won't tap it.

**Q:** If I can't attack with a just-summoned creature, or do anything else that would tap him, why don't you just say he's tapped on his first turn?

**A:** Because there are things he *can* do right away, like defend. He's not out of commission, he's just a little tired from the flight.

**Q:** When I regenerate a creature, it comes back tapped. Does that mean I can't do that on my creature's first turn out?

**A:** No. You may regenerate it. Tapping is an effect of regeneration, not part of the cost. This subtle difference also means that a creature can still regenerate even if it is already tapped.

**Q:** Are walls creatures? And can they be tapped?

**A:** Yes, and yes. Walls are creatures that lack the ability to attack. If they somehow become tapped, they can't block until they are untapped, just like any other creature.

**Q:** So, if they can't attack, why do some walls have power ratings?

**A:** Any defending creature deals damage equal to its

power rating to the creature(s) it blocks. The **Wall of Swords** is 3/5; this doesn't mean it can attack, it just means that any creature foolish enough to blunder into it will take 3 points of damage.

**Q:** Trample: **Mammoths** are 3/3, with trample. If I use them to defend against a 1/1 **Goblin,** does the extra damage carry over to the Goblin's controller?

**A:** No. Trample only works when they are attacking.

**Q:** Okay, now they're attacking. If they are blocked by two 1/1 Goblins, I get to assign the damage, right?

**A:** Yes, unless there is a banding creature among the goblins.

**Q:** Okay, forget about banding for a minute. Can I choose to damage only one of the Goblins, miss the other one, and let the other 2 points carry over to my opponent?

**A:** Yes. You could do the same type of assignment with a non-trampling creature, although the extra damage would not carry over.

**Q:** Suppose one of the Goblins above has the banding ability. Then what?

**A:** The only difference is that the defending player would get to distribute the damage however she wanted. If she only sacrificed one of her Goblins, 2 points of trample damage would still carry over.

**Q:** If there are several blockers, only *one* of them has to have the banding ability for this effect to occur?

**A:** That's right. And the damage can be allocated to any creatures in any amounts the defender wants.

**Q:** For attack or defense, when a flying creature bands with a non-flyer, can the band fly?

**A:** No. Banding attackers do not actually travel together; they just agree that if any one of them is stopped, the others will all rally round and help pound on the defender. If all of the creatures can slip past the defenders, because the individuals can fly, islandwalk or sneak invisibly past, then they'll do that. However, if one of the members of the band would be blocked, then the others won't abandon that member. They'll all fight together. Banding on the defending side is never declared; defenders block whatever they can, and then if there is at least one banding creature among those blocking a particular attacker, the defender distributes damage among those creatures.

**Q:** Can't the **Hero** ride on the **Pegasus**?

**A:** No. They are cards, not real creatures. The **Wolves** can't carry the **Sea Serpent** across dry land, either.

**Q:** Okay, so what good is banding again? It's beginning to sound pointless.

**A:** Banding allows the player to control where the damage goes. Creatures have to be blocked as one, or let through. The controller of the band gets to assign the damage it receives, not the other player.

Also, lots of little creatures can block together and foist *all* of the damage off on a particular partner they don't like, or one who can regenerate, or to one who is warded against the attacker's color, and they get to do all of their damage to the attacking creature. Sound better yet?

**Q:** How do other creature fast effects work?

**A:** See the **Timing** discussion above, and read the answers about the **Prodigal Sorcerer** that follow. Most Creature fast effects work like his.

**Q:** What's up with the **Prodigal Sorcerer?**

**A:** The **Prodigal Sorcerer** may be the single most asked-about card in **Magic**. The Sorcerer has a peculiar little fast effect that seems innocuous enough. There are other cards with similar effects, but the Prodigal Sorcerer is more common than most of them. Read through these answers even if you don't have a Prodigal Sorcerer, because all the answers about his abilities and timing apply to other, similar cards. Let's have a look at him: "Tap to do 1 damage to any target." This, like almost every creature special ability, is a fast effect, and can be played like an instant. See the timing rules above for more clarification.

(By the way, his nickname is Tim.)

**Q:** Tim is attacking. He's blocked. Now I want to use his special ability. Can I?

**A:** No, because he is already tapped from attacking.

You can't use his special ability or do anything else until he is untapped.

**Q:** Tim is blocking. Before damage is dealt, I decide to use his special ability. Now what happens?

**A:** The block still happens, but since Tim has become tapped, he deals no damage to the creature he blocked. He will still take damage from his attacker, though, unless that creature was killed before the damage-dealing phase.

**Q:** If my opponent's Tim tries to poke me, can I use my **Circle of Protection: Blue?**

**A:** Yes. As always with every time you use the Circle, it will cost you a point of mana. If another blue source tries to damage you, you need to power it again. If the same Tim somehow manages to untap and poke at you again, the Circle will cost another point to use.

**Q:** The **Nettling Imp** has a special power: it can force one of your opponent's creatures to attack. What if my opponent's Nettling Imp forces my **Prodigal Sorcerer** to attack?

**A:** The Imp card says that any creature which is unable to attack is destroyed (with certain exceptions). So you've got two alternatives:

> 1. Let the Sorcerer participate in the attack. This means he won't be able to use his special poke this turn, and he may be blocked by something nasty.

2. Tap the Sorcerer to do a point of damage (to the Imp, for example).

This response is a fast effect and happens simultaneously with the nettling; if the Imp dies, the Sorcerer is still affected by its power. Ergo, Tim will die from being unable to attack.

## Other Terms

**Q:** What *exactly* does "tapping" mean?

**A:** Tapping is the physical act of turning a card sideways. Untapping is the reverse. Tapping exists as a separate act from the actual use of a card; you simply tap a card to remind yourself that you've used it.

This means that tapping your opponent's card (through the use of spells, for example) does *not* give you control over the card's powers. It just means you're changing the card's orientation, which prevents it from being used. It doesn't force your opponent to use the card's powers. However (and this confuses a lot of players,) your opponent can tap the card for a fast effect, using the power before your tapping takes effect. (If you tap my **Orcs**, you don't get to attack with them, but neither do I.)

If you magically untap something in play, it may be used again.

Untapping an attacking creature doesn't prevent it from attacking; it just means that it suddenly feels fresh and good as new, and can be used for defense later if needed.

**Q:** **Psychic Venom** says I take a point of damage when the land is tapped. Is that true even when my opponent taps it with a spell?

**A:** Yes. The text specifically says, "Whenever target land is tapped."

**Q:** What's the "casting cost" of a spell?

**A:** To cast any spell, you have to spend mana points. These are denoted in the upper right-hand corner of the card, either in mana symbols, numbers, or both. Numbers in gray circles represent quantities of mana of any or no color, your choice.

**Q:** What about a card that refers to the casting cost of another card?

**A:** In that case, it's talking about the total number of mana points required. Color is irrelevant.

**Q:** When the card says it does damage to "any target," does that include my opponent?

**A:** Yes. If it says "target creature," then it can't be used on players. If it says "you," "your opponent," or "target player," then it can't be used on creatures.

**Q:** Are the terms "Kill" and "Destroy" synonymous?

**A:** Yes. In both cases, you may attempt to regenerate the creature being killed or destroyed.

**Q:** And "goes to the graveyard"?

**A:** This means that the card must be placed in the graveyard. Once a creature is Sacrificed, it must go to the graveyard, and can't be regenerated or other fancy stuff. **Protection, Guardian Beast, Consecrate Land,** and other protective effects cannot save cards that are sacrificed or "placed in the graveyard."

**Q:** What about "discarded"?

**A:** If it refers to a card in a player's hand, the card is simply placed in the graveyard and generates no effect. If it refers to a card in play, it's synonymous with "destroyed" and the card may be protected or regenerated.

**Q:** Are the terms "gone to the graveyard," "killed," "discarded," and "destroyed" synonymous?

**A:** These are all past tense. If a card actually goes into the discard pile, then it was killed/discarded/destroyed/sent to the graveyard.

The Revised rules have clearly defined "kill" and "destroy" as identical, and have replaced "destroyed without possibility of regeneration" with "buried." This saves space, and works for any type of card (instead of just creatures).

**Q:** What's the distinction between "controller," "owner," and "caster"?

**A:** A card's owner never changes through the course of the game, except through a few special ante spells. The caster or player of a card is the person who brings it into play. That also means the owner, even if his opponent forced him to play it. The controller of a card is the only thing which has much likelihood of changing.

- If you play a card, it remains under your control. If it's some sort of curse you've laid on your opponent, you're still the card's controller.

- This is true even if your opponent is required to pay the card's upkeep cost.

- Control only shifts when a particular card says so. Cards like Control Magic let you take control of your opponent's cards. Fork duplicates a spell and gives you control over that copy, regardless of who cast the original.

- Even if you have managed to steal a creature, you haven't taken control of its enchantments. If you steal a **Firebreathing Goblin,** you still can't pump up the firebreathing, although your opponent can.

When a card says "you," it's talking to its controller. When a card says "your" it refers to cards you control, regardless of who owns them.

**Q:** Can the X on an X-spell be zero?

**A:** Yes.

**Q:** So I can cast a zero-point Disintegrate?

**A:** You can if you want. And if that creature dies from something else this turn, it will still be removed from the game.

**Q:** I have a **Zombie Master** that makes Zombies in play get stronger. That just means *my* Zombies, right?

**A:** No. Any reference to "cards in play" is talking about all of them. This means you'll have to be a little more careful about how you use this card.

**Q:** Does this mean that when I cast a spell that "destroys all plains in play," that mine are destroyed as well?

**A:** Yes. Cards that are only specific to your opponent will say so. All means *all*.

**Q:** So, "Each Upkeep" means I have to deal with it during mine and my opponent's?

**A:** Oops, no. This card is talking to you. If the card affects both players, each must deal with it during his or her own Upkeep phase.

**Q:** Can I discard whenever I want to?

**A:** No. The only time you can discard is during your Discard phase, and then only if you have more than seven cards.

**Q:** Can I discard face down?

**A:** No. The Graveyard is still a semi-active source of cards, and you must let your opponent know what you've put into it.

**Q:** Suppose I don't want to draw. Can I skip my Draw phase?

**A:** No. And if you can't draw a card, you lose.

**Q:** The rules say that whenever a card contradicts the rules, the card takes precedence. What happens when two cards contradict each other?

**A:** If two enchantments on the same card contradict each other, the last one cast takes precedence. Other than that, if the rules don't cover it, you have to make a judgment call. No hierarchy has been designed to cover all possible infractions of the rules; this is by definition impossible.

**Q:** If it's impossible, what am I supposed to do?

**A:** Decide the answer for yourself or ask around. Chances are, it's come up before. It may even appear somewhere in a FAQ like this one. And it's possible that there is a simple rule you have overlooked.

## Miscellaneous Cards

**Q:** Chaos Orb: can I blow on it?

**A:** No. You can't tickle the caster either. Try telling a joke. Also, "turn over completely" means flipping, just like a coin, a full 360 degrees.

**Q:** Lich: My opponent keeps playing this on me. Is this fair?

**A:** Not at all. The card is an enchantment, and says, "You lose all life…" When a card refers to "you," it refers to the caster or controller of the card. Also, enchantments can only be played in the caster's territory unless the card says otherwise. He can only use it on himself. See the card to find out why he would…

**Q:** **Iron Star, Ivory Cup, Throne of Bone, Crystal Rod, Wooden Sphere:** These are essentially the same card, but for different colored spells. Can I use my Throne of Bone more than once to get several life points from the casting of a single black spell?

**A:** No. This is a little unclear in the shorthand on the cards. You may use it many times on each turn, but only once for each black spell.

**Q:** Okay, can I use my Throne of Bone to get a life point from a spell that was countered?

**A:** No.

**Q:** **Earthbind:** Does this card deal its damage each round?

**A:** No. Earthbind only damages a creature on the round it is cast. After that, the creature loses its flying ability.

**Q:** What if I cast a Flight enchantment on an Earthbound Flying creature?

**A:** The creature can fly again. Whenever two effects on a creature directly contradict each other, the last-used effect wins.

**Q: Raise Dead:** Can I get a dead thing out of my opponent's graveyard?

**A:** No. It specifically says "your graveyard." Even when this isn't the case, a card which just says "Graveyard" or "Library" is talking about yours. Animate Dead, on the other hand, lets you dig around in either graveyard.

**Q: Nevinyrral's Disk:** This is an artifact which destroys all creatures, enchantments, and artifacts in play, including itself. If my opponent uses his, and I've got **Elves** with a regeneration enchantment, what happens?

**A:** You can use the regeneration enchantment as it is destroyed, since both the Elves and the enchantment try to go to the graveyard at the same time. The enchantment saves the Elves, but nothing can save the enchantment. Result: Elves but no regeneration.

**Q: Double-Land Cards:** When I change the land type, what do they become?

**A:** It depends. You can't change just half of a First Edition double-land card, so it becomes a basic land of the appropriate type. If you're using Revised Edition rules, it depends on whether the effect that changes the land type is targeted or not. If the effect targets a specific land card, like Phantasmal Terrain and Evil Presence do, then the target double-land becomes a basic land of the appropriate type. If it's a mass effect that changes all mountains to plains, for example, it changes only the mountain half of a double-land, turning a Badlands (mountain and swamp) into a Scrubland (plains and swamp) and a Plateau into a basic plains.

**Q:** **Volcanic Eruption:** "Destroys X mountains of your choice, and does X damage to each player and each creature in play." Can I spend more X than there are mountains?

**A:** No.

**Q:** **Jade Statue:** I can temporarily turn this artifact into a creature. Can I attack with this on the turn I summon it?

**A:** No.

**Q:** Can I cast creature enchantments on it?

**A:** No. The statue says it can only be a creature during attack or defense. You can't cast enchantments during that time. It also can't be treated as a creature when it's in the Graveyard.

**Q:** **Clone:** Can I clone a **Doppleganger?**

**A:** Yes, and the Clone becomes a Doppleganger copying whatever the other Doppelganger was copying. It may switch independently during its next upkeep phase.

**Q:** What if my Doppleganger copies a Clone? Does it change color?

**A:** It can't; it copies whatever creature the Clone has become. There's really no such thing as a "Clone in play" because at the moment of summoning, the

Clone becomes in all respects a different creature.

**Q: Weakness:** If I play weakness (enchantment, −2/−1) on **Drudge Skeletons** (1/1, regenerating,) it will kill them. What if they are regenerated?

**A:** Regeneration preserves a creature's enchantments, even the ones you don't want. Once they're back, Weakness will kill them again. The cycle repeats until you can no longer afford to regenerate them.

**Q: Siren's Call** or **Nettling Imp:** I've got a card that forces other creatures to attack. I am supposed to play it during my opponent's turn, before he attacks. When I do that, what happens?

**A:** You force him to attack. But you don't force it to happen right away. You've only made sure that your opponent will have to attack sometime during this turn, and that the creature(s) you've affected will participate. Your opponent can still perform any other elements of the Main Phase before the attack is finally launched.

**Q: Swords To Plowshares:** This card gives a creature's controller life points based on the creature's power. That doesn't include enchantments, does it?

**A:** Actually it does. Cards like this refer to the creature's current power, including any enchantments on it, and any fast effects or other events which may occur before the spell is resolved.

**Q: Goblin King, Lord of Atlantis, Zombie Master:** These cards give special powers to other creatures I have in play. Do these cards affect themselves?

**A:** No. The Zombie Master isn't a Zombie, and so on.

**Q: Goblin Balloon Brigade:** Does this card make *all* Goblins flying, or just itself?

**A:** This is worded a little ambiguously. It can only float itself.

## Final Notes

**Q:** What's to keep somebody from spending piles of cash and making an enormous deck?

**A:** Game design. They can buy all the cards they want, but after a certain point they will just be able to build more decks, not better ones. Huge decks aren't really better either; there's a much higher chance that the cards you need will never come out.

**Q:** Some of my cards were mangled during manufacture. What do I do?

**A:** If you've got a damaged card, send it to us and we'll attempt to replace it. If it's rare, there may be a delay while we acquire a spare. If you were shorted cards, write us a letter and we'll send a random card for a replacement. For our latest official policy concerning manufacturing flaws, call or write. This policy can change depending on product availability.

**Q:** Can I get the original artwork?

**A:** A fantasy and science fiction art gallery called **Wizards**

(no relation) is the main source for **Magic** art. Contact them to see if they have the piece you want available:

Wizards Gallery
117 Main Street
Kirkland WA 98033
(206) 828–0237
@compuserve.com

Some artists are selling their work individually. Contact Wizards of the Coast if the gallery doesn't carry the artist in which you're interested.

**Q:** How do I get info faster?

**A:** The best source for answers to **Magic** questions is the Garfield Games mailing list. To subscribe, send an electronic mail message to listserv@wizards.com. The body of the message should contain the following line:

subscribe gg-l *your real name*

where *your real name* would be, for example, Pat Doe. Note that sending the subscription request (or unsubscription request) to gg-l@wizards.com won't do you any good, and will just annoy the subscribers.

If you want to trade cards, you'd want to send a message to listserv@wizards.com reading

subscribe gg-trading-l *your real name*

Again, note that sending the subscription (or unsubscription) request anywhere but to

```
listserv@wizards.com
```

is pointless, and just annoys people.

We have official representatives monitoring the RPG areas of Compuserve, America Online, and The Imagination Network; the Usenet newsgroup `rec.games.deckmaster`; and have an office building in Freegate, the MOO (MUD) at Illuminati Online. These are good places to look if you don't want to deal with the overflow of information on `gg-l`. You can also send questions to `questions@wizards.com`, but you'll probably get sent a copy of this FAQ unless it's a real puzzler.

If you don't intend to participate much in the discussions of **Magic**, you might want to subscribe to *Voices In My Head*, a digest of material from the networks compiled and edited into a weekly electronic magazine. Subscribe to this just like you'd subscribe to `gg-l`, except use `voices-l` as the list name.

For even more information, you can get a lot of interesting files from `marvin.macc.wisc.edu` by using anonymous FTP to retrieve files from that site's `/pub/deckmaster` directory.

# A Glossary of *Magic: The Gathering* Terms

The following definitions are brief explanations of terms commonly used in *Magic: The Gathering*. They are not meant to substitute for or supercede the complete Revised Edition rules contained in this book. In the case of any discrepancy, the rules take precedence over the glossary definition of any term.

**Activation cost:** the cost that must be paid to trigger an effect of an artifact, creature, or enchantment. Usually this cost is mana and/or tapping, but other costs are possible. Activation cost is written on the cards as *cost: effect*.

**Ante:** the stake in a **Magic** game (normally the top card of each player's deck).

**Artifact:** usually represents a magically powered object. An Artifact card does not become an Artifact until it is successfully cast.

**Artifact Creature:** an Artifact that is also a Creature; this might be a living statue or other such construction. Artifact Creatures are affected by anything that affects either Artifacts or Creatures, and follow all rules for both.

**Attack Phase:** the part of the turn during which Creatures attack the opposing sorcerer.

**Attacking Creature:** applies only during the Attack Phase. An attacking creature is any creature on the attacking side participating in the attack, whether tapped or not. Creatures not participating in the attack are not attacking creatures.

**Banding:** a special ability some creatures have that allows them to group with another creature while attacking, and to distribute damage differently when either attacking or defending.

**Basic Land:** Plains, Island, Swamp, Mountain, or Forest.

**Block, Blocked, Blocking:** Creatures cannot directly attack other creatures. When a creature attempts to attack the opposing player, that player can *block* with his own creatures. Attacking creatures that are opposed by a defending creature in this fashion are *blocked*. The defending creature is called a *blocking* creature.

**Buried:** killed/destroyed and sent to the Graveyard, without the possibility of Regeneration.

**Card:** any **Magic** card. This does not include creatures that are represented by tokens rather than cards.

**Caster:** the player who originally cast a spell, regardless of who currently controls the card.

**Characteristics (of a creature):** the type, color, power, toughness, casting cost, and special abilities of a creature. Any enchantments on the creature don't count toward its characteristics. The expansion symbol (such as the *Arabian Nights* scimitar) is not a Characteristic, and is not copied by a Clone.

**Color:** White, Blue, Black, Red, or Green. The color of a spell is normally determined by the color of mana used to cast the spell, but some spells may change the color of another spell or card. The borders of the cards indicate the color of a spell at a glance.

**Colorless:** a card or spell is *colorless* if it is neither white, blue, black, red, nor green. Artifacts and Lands are colorless. *Colorless mana* is produced by some artifacts. Many spells require mana of no specific color; this is also referred to as "colorless," and is represented by a gray circle with a number in it. These mana requirements can use any color of mana; they do *not* require the special colorless mana.

**Continuous:** effects that apply all the time. If there is no cost associated with an effect listed on a card, then it is continuous. Continuous effects of creatures and enchantments can only be stopped by getting rid of the card; continuous effects of artifacts stop while the artifact is tapped.

**Controller:** the player currently controlling a card in play. This is usually the player who cast the spell, but some spells can change the controller of a card.

**Cost (of a spell):** the amount of mana needed to cast the spell, shown in the upper right corner of the card. If a card refers to the "casting cost" of a spell, it means *only* the total number of mana points, not the color. The casting cost of non-card creatures is zero.

**Counter (1):** a marker used to keep track of charges or other special effects of a spell. These may take any form—pennies, stones, or even slips of paper with numbers written on them.

**Counter (2):** to cancel a spell before it can take effect. If a spell is countered, all mana used to cast it is wasted and the card goes to the Graveyard. Only an Interrupt can counter a spell.

**Creature:** a monster or other ally brought to the sorcerer's aid by a Summon spell. Note that some spells affect creatures and others affect spells. A "summon creature" card is a spell while being cast, and becomes a creature only after having been successfully cast.

**Creature Abilities:** any special effects listed in the text box of a creature card. Some abilities are common, and many creatures may have them; others are unique to one specific creature.

**Damage:** wounds or magically caused injuries. Creatures do damage when they attack, and many spells cause damage. Any time that a creature has damage equal to or exceeding its toughness, it is "killed." Each point of damage done to the player results in a loss of one life point unless prevented or redirected.

**Damage Dealing:** one of the steps in the Attack Phase, in which damage is assigned, and no fast effects may be used by either player.

**Damage Prevention:** the prevention/redirection of damage or regeneration of a creature assigned damage or on its way to the Graveyard. No fast effects other than prevent/redirect damage, regeneration or Interrupts may be used.

**Deck:** the set of cards a player uses for a game of **Magic**. Players select cards from their own collections to build decks with. A deck must contain at least forty cards; there is no maximum size.

**Defending Creature:** See *Blocking*. In the Revised Edition, *defending creature* is synonymous with *blocking creature*. In the First Edition, defending creature meant any creature on the defending side during the attack phase, whether blocking or not.

**Discard (1):** take a card from your hand and put it in your Graveyard.

**Discard (2):** When referring to a card in play, read "discard" as "destroy." It may be saved by Regeneration, where-upon it does not count as a "discarded card."

**Destroyed:** sent to the Graveyard, but may be saved by Regeneration. If the card is a Creature, this is synonymous with Killed.

**Dominia:** the multiverse in which **Magic** duels take place.

**Duel:** a single game of **Magic**.

**Enchantment:** one of the basic spell types. An enchant-ment remains in play permanently unless it (or the object it is enchanting) is destroyed. Enchantments may only be cast during your own turn, during the Main phase.

**Evasion Abilities:** creature abilities that prevent a crea-ture from being blocked during the Attack phase. The most common evasion abilities are Flying and Landwalk.

**Fast Effect:** interrupts, instants, and non-continuous effects of permanents. Unless otherwise specified on the card, you can use fast effects at any time during any player's turn except the damage-dealing subphase.

**First Strike:** a special ability some creatures have, which allows them to do their damage first. If a First Strike crea-ture faces a normal creature, the First Striker may be able to kill its opponent and take no damage in return.

**Flying:** a creature with the Flying ability can only be blocked by other Flying creatures. Flying creatures *can* block non-Flying creatures; they just can't be blocked by them.

**Graveyard:** the discard pile. Each player has a separate Graveyard pile. Cards discarded from your hand, expended spells, and creatures killed in play all go to their owner's Graveyard. Cards in the Graveyard do not retain any enchantments, counters, or other attributes acquired before the card was placed in the Graveyard.

**Hand:** the cards a player has drawn from their Library but not yet played. Cards in your hand are just cards; they become spells at the time you attempt to cast them, and may become creatures, artifacts, or enchantments if the casting succeeds.

**Instant:** one of the basic spell types. Instants have effects that last for a limited time; if not otherwise specified, all instants wear off at the end of the turn. The card for an instant spell is placed in your Graveyard as soon as the spell is successfully cast.

**Interrupt:** one of the basic spell types. Unlike instants, the effects of an interrupt are permanent, though the card is still placed in your Graveyard as soon as the spell is successfully cast. Only an interrupt can prevent a fast effect from occurring.

**Kill:** remove a creature from play and place it in the Graveyard. Unless the card specifies otherwise, this death can be prevented by Regeneration.

**Land:** cards in **Magic** come in two types: land and spells. Most land provides mana, but some land cards have other special abilities.

**Landwalk:** the evasion abilities Swampwalk, Mountain-walk, etc. A creature with *Landtype*walk cannot be blocked if the defender has any lands of type *Landtype* in play.

**Library:** the pile of cards you draw from when playing **Magic**.

**Life (Life Point):** each player starts with 20 life points. Each point of damage done to the player subtracts 1 life point if not prevented or redirected. If a player has less than 1 life point at the end of a phase or start or end of an attack, that player loses the duel.

**Main Phase:** the part of your turn when you can cast enchantments and sorceries, play land, and attack your opponent.

**Mana:** the energy that powers spells in **Magic**. Most mana comes from land, but some artifacts, spells, and creatures can also produce mana.

**Mana Pool:** the mana you have available for casting a spell. When you draw mana from lands or other sources, it goes into your mana pool. In order to cast a spell, you must have sufficient mana of the proper colors in your mana pool to cover the cost of the spell. Mana left in your mana pool at the end of a phase or at the start or end of an attack is wasted and causes damage to you.

**Owner:** the real-life owner of a card, as opposed to the player who happens to be controlling it at a given point in the game. (If you're borrowing cards from a friend to play with, you're still considered the "owner" for game purposes.)

**Permanent:** a card that remains in play after being used. Lands, artifacts, creatures, and enchantments are all permanents once in play. Note that the spell must be successfully cast before it becomes a permanent; while being cast, it is just a spell.

**Phase:** each player's turn in **Magic** is broken down into several parts, called phases. Each of these phases happens every turn, although in any given turn nothing may actually occur during certain phases.

**Power:** the amount of damage a creature can do in a normal attack. Each creature card has two numbers in the bottom right corner; the first number is the creature's power, the second is its toughness.

**Protection:** a creature with Protection from a particular color of magic cannot be damaged, blocked, or targeted by creatures and effects of that color, but is still vulnerable to non-targeted, non-damaging effects.

**Regeneration:** a fast effect that saves a creature on the verge of death, just before it goes to the Graveyard. Some creatures have a built-in ability to regenerate. Creatures that are "killed" or "destroyed" may regenerate, but creatures that are "buried" or "removed from the game" may not.

**Removed from Game:** a few spells can cause a card to be removed completely from the game. Instead of putting the card in your Graveyard, set it aside; you can't shuffle it back into your deck or otherwise use it until the duel is over.

**Sacrifice:** remove one of your cards from play and place it in your Graveyard. This removal may not be prevented, even by effects that would normally prevent a card from being damaged or destroyed. If an effect calls for a sacrifice, you may sacrifice any card that you control, whether or not you own it.

**Sorcery:** one of the basic spell types. Like instants, sorceries take effect as soon as they are successfully cast, and the card is placed in the Graveyard immediately after being cast. However, sorceries may only be cast during your own turn, during the main phase.

**Source:** the *source* of damage is the creature or card that caused that damage. Damage is considered to be the same color as its source. The source of damage from unspent mana is your mana pool; this damage is colorless.

**Special Ability:** see *Creature Ability*.

**Spell:** cards in **Magic** come in two types: land and spells. Some cards bring a creature or artifact into play; these cards are considered spells while being cast, and creatures or artifacts only if the casting finishes successfully.

**Summon:** to bring a creature into play by means of a Summoning spell. Summon Creature cards are treated as spells while being cast; if the casting is successful, the card then represents the creature that was summoned.

**Tap:** to mark a card or token as used, normally by turning it sideways. Many cards with special abilities require tapping the card as part or all of the cost for that ability. Note that tapping the card does not in itself generate the effect; rather, generating the effect causes the card to be tapped.

**Tapped:** turned sideways, marked as having been used. Artifacts with continuous effects have no effect while they are tapped, but creature special effects still work even while tapped.

**Target:** the card, token, or player that a spell is aimed at. If a spell allows free choice of targets, it can affect any creature or player of your choice. Some spells have no target: for example, spells that affect an entire category of creatures.

**Territory:** the area you play your cards in is called your territory. Each player has their own territory.

**Token:** any object used to represent a creature created by a spell that has no card of its own. Spells that affect "cards" don't affect tokens.

**Toughness:** the amount of damage it takes to kill a creature. Each Creature card has two numbers in the bottom right corner; the first number is the creature's power, the second is its toughness.

**Trample:** a special ability some creatures have, allowing them to damage a player even when blocked provided that they have more than enough power to kill the blocker.

**Trample Damage:** damage done by an attacking creature with the Trample special ability. Trample damage is always applied after normal damage. In the damage-dealing subphase, any points of trample damage on a creature above that creature's toughness are applied to the creature's controller.

**Turn:** a single player's turn, beginning with untapping cards and ending with clearing all damage to creatures. When one player's turn finishes, the next player's turn begins. Some spells may be used during any player's turn; others may only be played during your own turn. Any effects that happen "each turn" affect each player during his own turn.

**Untap (1):** to turn a card back to the normal position, marking it as available for use. Note that untapping a card does not undo any of its effects.

**Untap (2):** the first phase in a player's turn in which all of the player's cards must be untapped (see **Untap 1**) unless specifically prevented from doing so. This phase is assumed to occur instantaneously; therefore, no fast effects or other cards may be used by either player during this phase.

**Upkeep:** the phase immediately after Untap. This is when damage that happens "at the beginning of the turn" takes effect, and when spells with upkeep costs must be paid for.

**Walk:** see *Landwalk*.

**Wall:** a special type of creature. Walls may not attack, even if they have a Power greater than zero. They are treated exactly as creatures for all other purposes, and may be affected by any spells that affect creatures.

**X:** some spells have an X in their casting cost. This X can stand for any number of mana points, even zero; the text on the card will explain any requirements for what X must be for that particular spell.

**You, Your:** cards that use "you" or "your" in their text mean the current controller of the card. This is usually, but not always, the player who cast the spell.

# Index

# DUELISTS'

## CONVOCATION™

### M E M B E R S H I P

Annual Membership Fee : $18 US
Make check or money order payable to
**Wizards of the Coast**   P.O. Box 707 Renton WA 98057

Name:_____

Date of Birth:_____/_____/_____

Mailing Address:_____

City_____State_____Zip_____

Phone: (_____)_____

_____     _____
Your Signature                 Parent/Guardian Signature
                               ( If you are under eighteen years of age)

| Date Filed: | Membership #: |
|---|---|
| Received by: | Payment Method: |

Office Use Only

# Deckmaster™ Customer Survey

Name: _____

Address: _____

_____

City                    State           Zip          Country

Phone ( _____ ) _____ -- _____

(We appreciate your response to this survey. It will help us design
better products and produce them in quantities which meet market
demand. Your answers will be treated as confidential.)

| I am primarily a: | (optional) | | |
|---|---|---|---|
| ☐ Card collector | Age | Sex | Annual income |
| ☐ Card/game player | ☐ under 15 | ☐ female | ☐ <$5000 |
| ☐ Roleplayer | ☐ 15-20 | ☐ male | ☐ $5-15,000 |
| ☐ Avid reader | ☐ 21-30 | | ☐ $15-30,000 |
| ☐ Other: _____ | ☐ 31-45 | | ☐ >$30,000 |
| | ☐ over 45 | | |

Type/approx. # of **Deckmaster™** products I have purchased:

( Approx. # of cards ) _____ **Magic: The Gathering™**

( Approx. # of cards ) _____ **Magic expansions**

( # of magazines ) _____ **The Duelist™**

( # of books ) _____ **Pocket Players' Guide™**

Favorite product: _____

Least favorite product: _____

**Pocket Players' Guide™ feedback:**
What I liked most: _____
What I disliked most: _____
I suggest these improvements: _____

_____

**Deckmaster™ feedback:**
I am_____ / am not_____ a member of the Duelists' Convocation.
I have been playing **Magic** for_____ months. I play_____ times/month.
Other games I play include: _____.

Please send completed survey to:

Wizards of the Coast
P.O. Box 707
Renton, WA 98057-9916